Oxford Skills World
Reading with Writing 2

Kathryn O'Dell

OXFORD
UNIVERSITY PRESS

OXFORD
UNIVERSITY PRESS

198 Madison Avenue
New York, NY 10016 USA

Great Clarendon Street, Oxford, OX2 6DP, United Kingdom

Oxford University Press is a department of the University of Oxford.
It furthers the University's objective of excellence in research, scholarship,
and education by publishing worldwide. Oxford is a registered trade
mark of Oxford University Press in the UK and in certain other countries

ISBN: 978 0 19 411348 9 Student Book with Workbook

Printed in China

This book is printed on paper from certified and well-managed sources

ACKNOWLEDGMENTS

*Oxford University Press would like to thank all of the teachers whose opinions helped to
inform this series, and in particular, the following reviewers:* Soo Ah Chung, Hwarang
Elementary School; Marta Juanet, Betania-patmos; Sedef Toksöz Kaykın,
Denizli Pamukkale Unv Egitim Vakfi okullari (PEV Koleji); Jeehee Moon,
T.T.R.; Jacob Rod, WILS Language School; Yuechun Wang, Phonenix City
International School

Cover illustration and main character illustrations by: Shane McGowan/The
Organisation

Back cover photograph: Oxford University Press building/David Fisher

Student Book

Illustrations by: David Arumi/Astound pp.65, 67; Robin Boyer/Illustration Online
pp.36, 44, 82; Mike Byrne/Advocate-Art pp.83, 84, 85; Mattia Cerato/MB Artists
pp.18, 55, 56; Charlene Chua pp.23, 24, 25, 46, 72; Pascale Constantin pp.12,
30, 42, 54, 78; Peter Francis/MB Artists pp.27, 29; John Kurtz p.16; Anthony
Lewis/MB Artists pp.11, 26, 52, 68, 80; Steffane McClary/Maggie-Byers-
Sprinzeles pp.37, 38; Jomike Tejido/MB Artists pp.13, 15, 81

Commissioned photography by: Oxford University Press: p.9 (paperclip bird)

*The Publishers would like to thank the following for their kind permission to reproduce
photographs and other copyright material:* 123rf: pp.8 (girl smiling/Sergey Novikov),
(art supplies/Gennadiy Poznyakov), 9 (paper clip/Worrapol Koranuntachai),
10 (paper clips/radub85), (child's bedroom/iriana88w), 12 (girl hitting piñata/
Cathy Yeulut), 13 (calendar/Takashi Honma), (ball of yarn/Anton Starikov),
14 (pencil sharpener/sirylok), (digital clock/Olga Papova), (ball of yarn/
belka10), 22 (toy store interior/赵 建康), 27 (action figure/ctrphotos), (wrist
watch/prapan Ngawkeaw), 28 (black wallet/Sergey Peterman), (action figure/
ctrphotos), 32 (action figure/ctrphotos), 34 (children playing tug-of-war/
wavebreakmedia), 39 (soccer ball/Tividar Geiner), 40 (children art class/
Antonio Diaz), (art and craft market/ojogabanitoo), 41 (children karate class/
Aleksey Satyrenko), 43 (jump rope/serezniy), (karate belts/hxdbzxy), (bicycle/
gemenacom), 50 (Tokyo/sean pavone), 55 (male police officer/Andrey Bayda),
(male firefighter/Flashon Studio), 66 (red grapes/svl861), 68 (berry smoothie/
Lecic), 69 (pasta with red sauce/Piotr Krzelak), (spaghetti/Gabor Havasi),
70 (brown rice/vitawin choomanee), (steak being grilled/Joshua Resnick),
(pasta in bowl/Piotr Krzelak), 71 (rice in bowl/Suphakaln Wongcompune),
(stew in bowl/David Kadlec), (steak/monphoto), 79 (boy brushing teeth/
Samantha Ireland), 82 (girl in science class/Rob Marmion), 83 (boy doing
homework/Jean-Paul CHASSENET), (girl watching television/Andriy Popov),
(girl in bed/PaylessImages); Alamy: pp.6-7 (children making art/Indiapicture),
64 (boy with doughnut/thislife pictures), (boy drinking juice/OJO Images
ltd), 65 (sandwich/Gabe Palmer), (burger/Ekaterina Khabieva), 66 (orange
cheese/Foodstock), (burger/Richard Griffin), 76-77 (children in bunk beds/
View Stock), 79 (father and daughter/Image Source), 86 (girl with television
remote/Blend Images), 88 (family eating dinner/Yooniq Images); Getty: Cover
(boy on bicycle/Sollina Images/Blend Images LLC), pp.8 (woman and girl in
hospital/Hero Images), 14 (calendar/peepo), 23 (child buying something/
KidStock), 37 (girl dancing/Jade Albert Studio, Inc.), 41 (girl jumping rope/
Tom Merton), (girl doing karate/FatCamera), 48-49 (father applying bandaid
to child/KidStock), 51 (multiple professions/Caiaimage/Martin Barraud),
58 (female animal dentist/Jan Otto), 60 (doctor shaking hands/Caiaimage/Paul
Bradbury), 62-63 (school cafeteria/asiseeit), 74 (boy eating pizza/KidStock),
79 (child waking up/somethingway); Oxford University Press: p.27 (candy
bar/Dennis Kitchen Studio, Inc); Shutterstock: pp.8 (girl painting sun/Syda
Productions), 9 (painting of nature/zorina_larisa), (glue bottle/BW Folsom),
(window/Peyker), 10 (picture of house/Hoika Mikhail), (glue bottle/BW
Folsom), 13 (pencil sharpener/oraveepix), (analog clock/Gavran333), 19 (pencil,
reused on pp.33, 47, 61, 75/almaje), 20 (girls in toy store/Kzenon), 23 (key
chain/Stratos Giannikos), (lunch box/MvanCaspel), (comic book/benchart),
26 (colourful dolls/gary yim), 27 (brown wallet/kocetoiliev), 28 (purple watch/
dmytro herasymeniuk), (unwrapped candy bar/Roman Samokhin), 36 (girl
kicking soccer ball/Amy Myers), 37 (boy swimming/Samuel Micut), (girl
skipping/Kichigin), (boy singing/BonD80), 39 (ballet shoes/Oscar Espinosa),
(skipping/Kichigin), (microphone/Laborant), 40 (children on scooters/
Romrodphoto), (boy swimming/sir.chitvises), 41 (children playing hopscotch/
Sergey Novikov), (boy riding bicycle/Collin Quinn Lomax), 43 (hopscotch
grid/Joel Blit), 50 (family in restaurant/Monkey Business Images), (hospital
corridor/wavebreakmedia), (parent's with child/Monkey Business Images),
51 (female dentist/wavebreakmedia), (female doctor/Africa Studio), (male vet/
Byelikova Oksana), (female cook/kurhan), 53 (female dentist/michaeljung),
(male cook/Minerva Studio), (female vet/didesign021), (male doctor/Minerva
Studio), 55 (male soccer player/Syda Productions), (female taxi driver/Africa
Studio), 64 (girl with strawberries/thitiwat chirayutwibul), (pizza and juice/
Africa Studio), 65 (yellow cheese/Artbox), (white grapes/Roxana Bashyrova),
66 (toasted sandwich/Olga Nayashkova), 69 (pasta with white sauce/Kris Tan),
(steak on plate/mikeledray), (stew/Olga Miltsova), (rice/espies), 70 (stew in
bowl/alisafarov), 71 (pasta with white sauce/Kris Tan), 79 (toddler sleeping/
mmaja), (girl on school bus/Monkey Business Images), 83 (boy eating dinner/
Africa Studio)

Workbook

Illustrations by: Mattia Cerato/MB Artists p.106; Anthony Lewis/MB Artists
p.92 (Ex 2a, Ex 3b)

*The Publishers would like to thank the following for their kind permission to reproduce
photographs and other copyright material:* 123rf: pp.91 (girl hitting piñata/Cathy
Yeulut), 92 (paper clip/Worrapol Koranuntachai), 94 (ball of yarn/Anton
Starikov), (calendar/Takashi Honma), 96 (paper clip/Worrapol Koranuntachai),
97 (toy store interior/赵 建康), 98 (action figure/ctrphotos), 100 (girl smiling/
Sergey Novikov), 104 (male police officer/Andrey Bayda), (male firefighter/
Flashon Studio), 105 (male firefighter/Flashon Studio), 108 (steak on grill/
Joshua Resnick), (berry smoothie/Lecic), 109 (park/silverjohn), 110 (spaghetti/
Gabor Havasi), 112 (boy brushing teeth/Samantha Ireland), 114 (girl watching
television/Andriy Popov), (boy doing homework/Jean-Paul CHASSENET),
(girl in bed/PaylessImages); Alamy: pp.92 (children making art/Indiapicture),
108 (burger/Ekaterina Khabieva), (sandwich/Gabe Palmer), 112 (father and
daughter/Image Source); Getty: pp.96 (girl buying something/KidStock),
100 (girl dancing/Jade Albert Studio, Inc.), (girl doing karate/FatCamera),
(girl buying something/KidStock), 102 (girl jumping rope/Tom Merton), (girl
doing karate/FatCamera), 112 (child waking up/somethingway), (girl doing
karate/FatCamera), (girl jumping rope/Tom Merton); Oxford University
Press: pp.98 and 108 (candy bar/Dennis Kitchen Studio, Inc); Shutterstock:
pp.92 (painting of nature/zorina_larisa), (window/Peyker), (glue bottle/
BW Folsom), 93 (doll/Nadiia Korol), 94 (analog clock/Gavran333), (pencil
sharpener/oraveepix), 95 (lunch box/MvanCaspel), 96 (window/Peyker),
(painting of nature/zorina_larisa), (comic book/benchart), (key chain/Stratos
Giannikos), (analog clock/Gavran333), (lunch box/MvanCaspel), 98 (purple
watch/dmytro herasymeniuk), (brown wallet/kocetoiliev), 99 (girl kicking
soccer ball/Amy Myers), 100 (children playing hopscotch/Sergey Novikov),
(boy singing/BonD80), (girl skipping/Kichigin), (boy swimming/Samuel Micut),
101 (hopscotch grid/Joel Blit), 102 (boy riding bicycle/Collin Quinn Lomax),
(children playing hopscotch/Sergey Novikov), 103 (female doctor/Africa
Studio), 104 (male doctor/Minerva Studio), (female dentist/wavebreakmedia),
(male soccer player/Syda Productions), (female vet/didesign021), (male cook/
Minerva Studio), (female taxi driver/Africa Studio), 107 (toasted sandwich/Olga
Nayashkova), 108 (yellow cheese/Artbox), (white grapes/Roxana Bashyrova),
(lunch box/MvanCaspel), 110 (white rice/espies), (steak on plate/mikeledray),
(stew/Olga Miltsova), 111 (girl on school bus/Monkey Business Images),
112 (boy riding bicycle/Collin Quinn Lomax), (girl on school bus/Monkey
Business Images), (children playing hopscotch/Sergey Novikov), 113 (girl in
superhero costume/Rawpixel.com), 114 (boy eating dinner/Africa Studio)

Table of Contents

Hi! I'm Olly.

Hi, I'm Molly!

Introduction

Welcome to Oxford Skills World

Oxford Skills World: Reading with Writing is a flexible paired skills course that takes students on a journey toward independent learning, providing them with strategies and support to reach their goals.

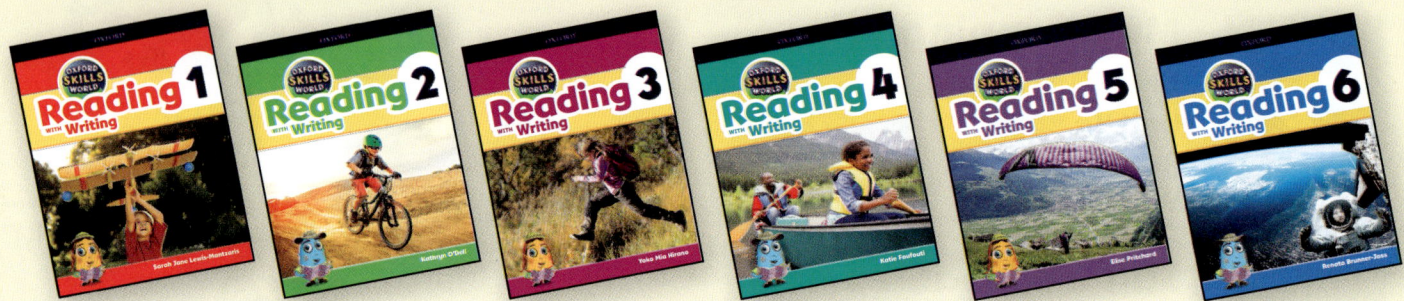

For Students

- Student Book / Workbook
- Student's website with downloadable audio and extra resources
  www.oup.com/elt/oxfordskillsworld

For Teachers

- Downloadable Teacher's Pack with instructional support, assessment, professional development videos, projects, and writing resources
- Classroom Presentation Tool
- Teacher's website with downloadable audio and extra resources
  www.oup.com/elt/teacher/oxfordskillsworld

Be the Leader on Your Skills Adventure!

Hi! We're Olly and Molly, your skills adventure guides. We help you reach your goals by introducing new reading and writing strategies, asking helpful questions, and giving friendly reminders. Most importantly, we cheer you on every step of the way! Let's go!

Quick Guide

Inside Each Topic

Topic Opener

Theme-based topics provide high-interest content relevant to students' lives.

My Goals introduces students to the objectives of each unit in the topic.*

Fun characters, Olly and Molly, encourage 21st century skills like critical thinking, collaboration, and communication.

Students answer questions to activate prior knowledge and think critically.

Get Ready to Read • Read

Reading Goals are strategies students can apply to any text.

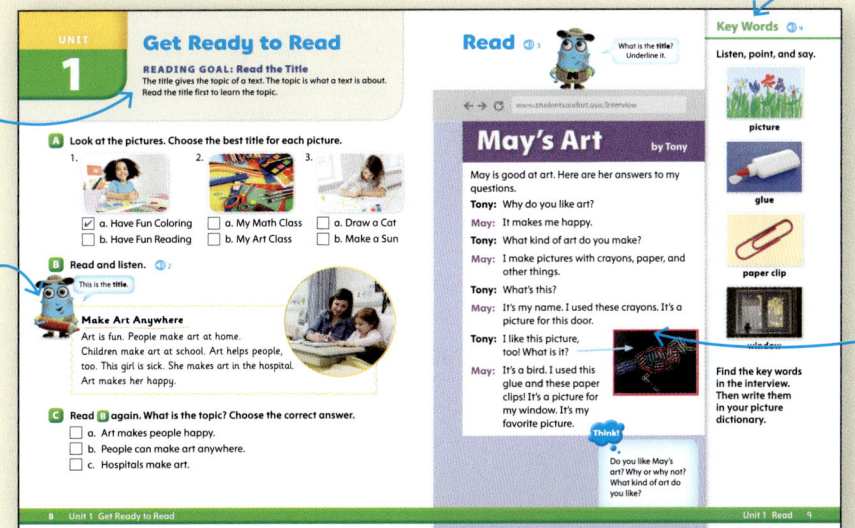

Students learn new vocabulary for each text and complete the picture dictionary at the back of the book.

Olly and Molly guide students as they learn and apply new reading strategies.

Students apply strategies to high-interest fiction and nonfiction texts, think critically about what they read, and make connections to their own lives.

*Each topic contains two thematically related units.

Quick Guide

Understand

Students increase their comprehension of the text by applying reading strategies to what they have read.

Students complete activities to strengthen their understanding of the unit's vocabulary.

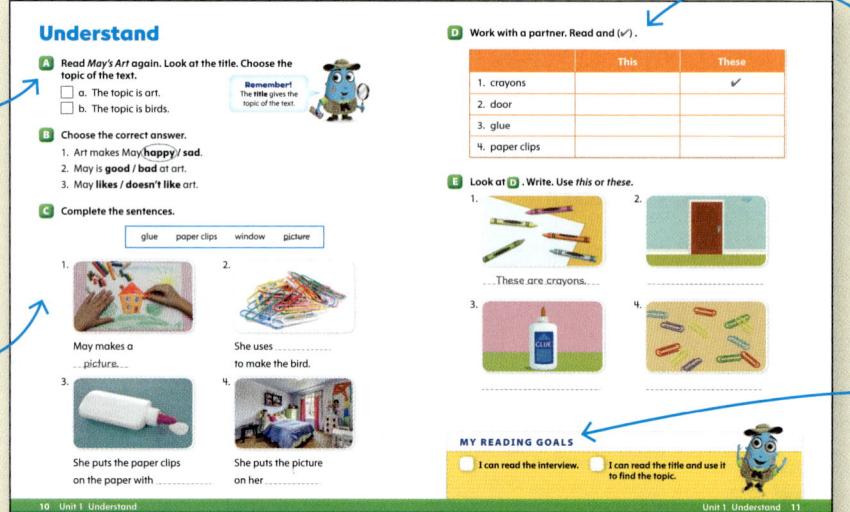

Students demonstrate comprehension of the unit's text, vocabulary, and grammar.

At the end of each unit, students assess the progress they have made toward achieving their goals.

Reading Check

With helpful reminders from Olly and Molly, students apply the **Reading Goals** from both units to a new text.

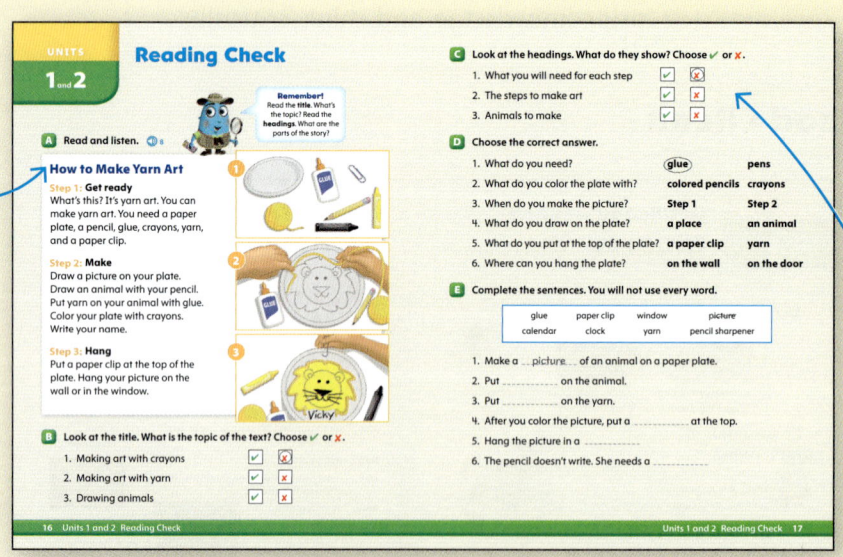

Students complete activities to boost comprehension and vocabulary application.

Get Ready to Write • Write

Writing Goals prepare students to write in different genres.

Writing Tips provide guidance on grammar, punctuation, and mechanics and help students write fluently and accurately.

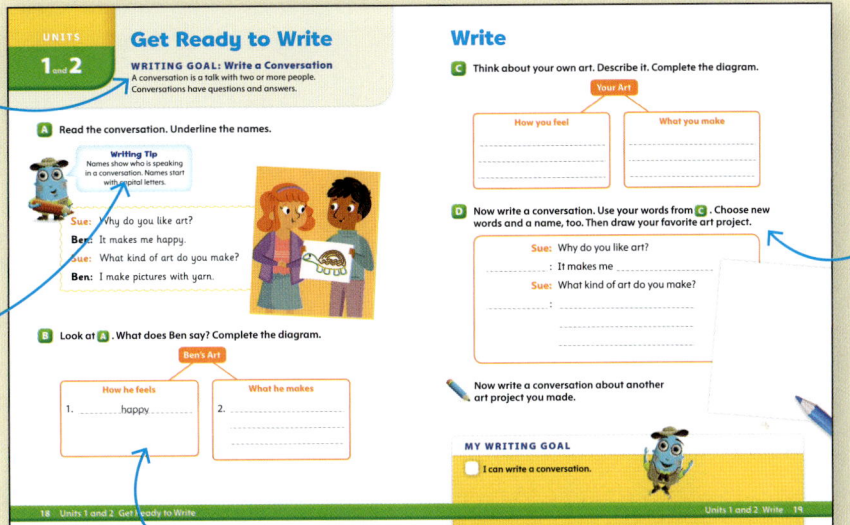

Scaffolded writing passages help students accomplish their writing goals.

Students use graphic organizers to comprehend model writing texts and to organize their thoughts for their own writing.

Workbook

Workbook pages at the end of the book provide more opportunities for students to apply their **Reading Goals** and boost comprehension.

Additional activities provide extra opportunities for vocabulary comprehension and usage.

Students apply the topic's **Writing Tip** to ensure proper usage in their own writing.

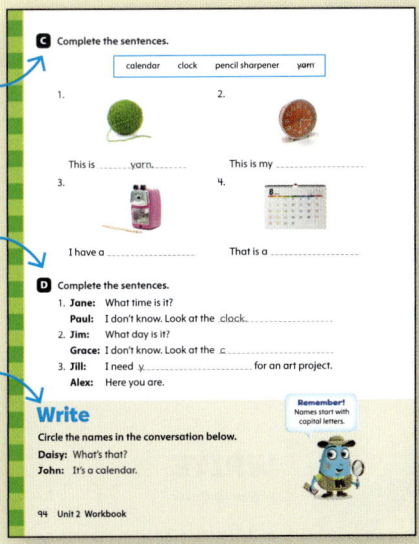

Art Smart

MY GOALS

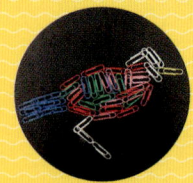

UNIT 1

- Read the interview *May's Art*
- Read the title

UNIT 2

- Read the story *Peter's Art Project*
- Read the headings

WRITE

- Write a conversation

A Look at the picture. What do you see?

1. What are the children doing?
2. Do you like their art? Why or why not?

B Read the Fun Fact. Then answer the questions.

1. How many words can you write with one pencil?

2. How many pencils do you have?

Think, Pair, Share
What art do you make?

Get Ready to Read

READING GOAL: Read the Title
The title gives the topic of a text. The topic is what a text is about.
Read the title first to learn the topic.

A Look at the pictures. Choose the best title for each picture.

1.

☑ a. Have Fun Coloring
☐ b. Have Fun Reading

2.

☐ a. My Math Class
☐ b. My Art Class

3.

☐ a. Draw a Cat
☐ b. Make a Sun

B Read and listen. 🔊 2

This is the **title**.

Make Art Anywhere

Art is fun. People make art at home.
Children make art at school. Art helps people,
too. This girl is sick. She makes art in the hospital.
Art makes her happy.

C Read **B** again. What is the topic? Choose the correct answer.

☐ a. Art makes people happy.

☐ b. People can make art anywhere.

☐ c. Hospitals make art.

Read  3

What is the **title**? Underline it.

← → ↻ www.studentsandart.osw/interview

May's Art
by Tony

May is good at art. Here are her answers to my questions.

Tony: Why do you like art?

May: It makes me happy.

Tony: What kind of art do you make?

May: I make pictures with crayons, paper, and other things.

Tony: What's this?

May: It's my name. I used these crayons. It's a picture for this door.

Tony: I like this picture, too! What is it?

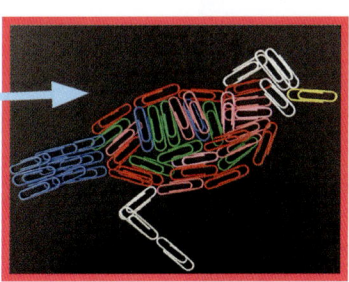

May: It's a bird. I used this glue and these paper clips! It's a picture for my window. It's my favorite picture.

Think!

Do you like May's art? Why or why not? What kind of art do you like?

Listen, point, and say.

picture

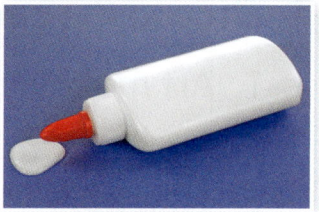

glue

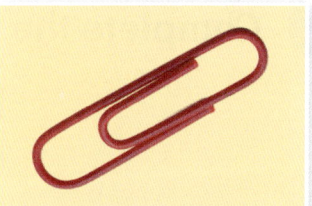

paper clip

window

Find the key words in the interview. Then write them in your picture dictionary.

Understand

A Read *May's Art* again. Look at the title. Choose the topic of the text.

Remember!
The **title** gives the topic of the text.

☐ a. The topic is art.

☐ b. The topic is birds.

B Choose the correct answer.

1. Art makes May (happy) / **sad**.

2. May is **good / bad** at art.

3. May **likes / doesn't like** art.

C Complete the sentences.

| glue | paper clips | window | ~~picture~~ |

1.

May makes a

___picture.___

2.

She uses _____

to make the bird.

3.

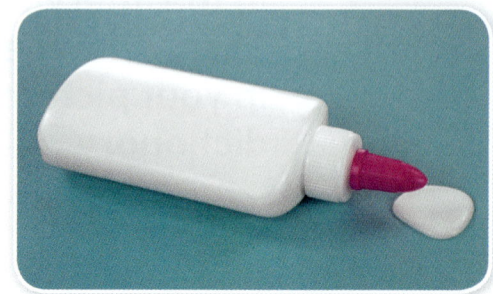

She puts the paper clips

on the paper with _____

4.

She puts the picture

on her _____

D Work with a partner. Read and (✔) .

	This	These
1. crayons		✔
2. door		
3. glue		
4. paper clips		

E Look at **D**. Write. Use *this* or *these*.

1.

These are crayons.

2.

_____

3.

_____

4.

_____

MY READING GOALS

☐ I can read the interview.　　☐ I can read the title and use it to find the topic.

Get Ready to Read

READING GOAL: Read the Headings

Headings show different parts of a text. Headings tell what each part is about. Read the headings first to learn about the different parts of the text.

A Look at the pictures and headings. What happens first? Order the headings.

Giving Dad a card

Making a card

1

Buying paper

B Read and listen. 🔊 5

These are **headings**.

The Piñata Party
by Ana Ortiz

Making a piñata

Making a piñata is easy. I use paper, glue, and paint.

Filling a piñata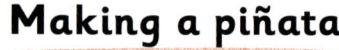

Is this candy? Yes, it is! I put candy in my piñata.

Breaking a piñata

At my party, my friends hit my piñata. Then I break it!

C Read **B** again. What happens first? Number the sentences.

Ana fills the piñata with candy. ☐

Ana breaks the piñata. ☐

Ana makes a piñata. 1

Read  🔊 6

Find the **headings**. What do you think the parts of the story are about?

Peter's Art Project

Monday morning

This is Peter. He looks at the calendar. He needs a picture for art class on Tuesday.

Monday afternoon

Peter uses a pencil sharpener. He's ready. What can he draw?

Monday evening

Peter doesn't know what to draw. He looks at the clock. Tick-tock. Tick-tock. It's late.

Monday night

Peter still doesn't know what to draw. He sees a bird by the window. The bird sings! Peter has an idea. He draws the bird. He puts yarn on his picture. He's very happy.

Think!

What does Peter draw for art class? Why?

Listen, point, and say.

calendar

pencil sharpener

clock

yarn

Find the key words in the story. Then write them in your picture dictionary.

Understand

Remember! **Headings** tell us about the parts of the story.

A Read *Peter's Art Project* again. Choose **Yes** or **No**.

1. The parts of the story are about what happens on Monday.   (Yes)   No

2. The story happens in one day.   **Yes**   **No**

3. Peter draws a picture before dinner.   **Yes**   **No**

B Choose the correct answer.

1. When is Peter's art class?

☐ a. Monday   ✔ b. Tuesday

2. Where is Peter?

☐ a. at school   ☐ b. at home

3. What does Peter use for his picture?

☐ a. a pencil and yarn   ☐ b. a crayon and a paper clip

4. What does Peter draw?

☐ a. a bird   ☐ b. a window

C Complete the sentences with key words. Then match.

1. This is a _pencil sharpener_ for pencils.

2. This is a _____. It's Monday.

3. That is a _____. It's late.

4. That is a ball of _____

a.

b.

c.

d.

_____1_____   _____   _____   _____

D Read *Peter's Art Project* again. When does Peter do these things? Work with a partner. Complete the timeline.

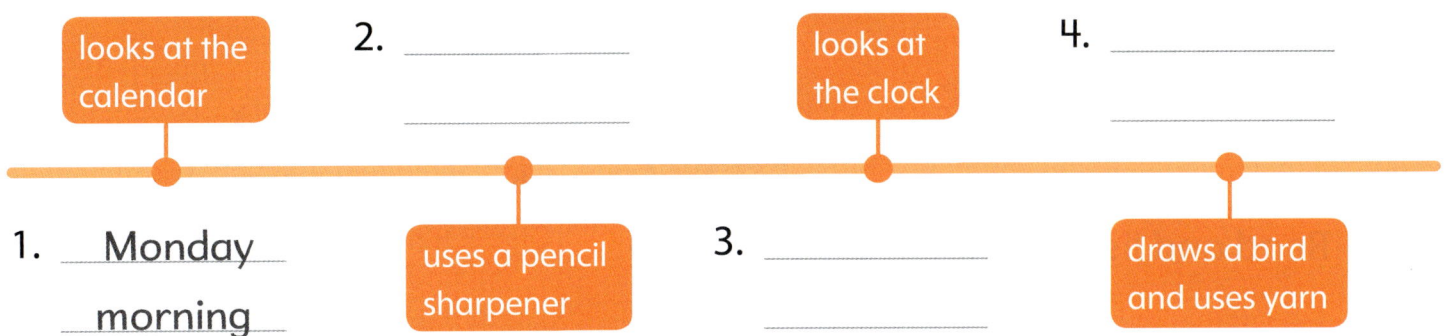

looks at the calendar

2. _____

_____

looks at the clock

4. _____

_____

1. ___Monday___

___morning___

uses a pencil sharpener

3. _____

_____

draws a bird and uses yarn

E Look at **D**. Write.

1.

Peter ___looks at a calendar___

on _____Monday morning._____

2.

He _____

on _____

3.

He _____ on

_____

4.

He _____

and _____

on _____

MY READING GOALS

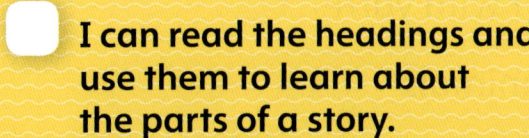

☐ I can read the story.

☐ I can read the headings and use them to learn about the parts of a story.

Reading Check

Remember!
Read the **title**. What's the topic? Read the **headings**. What are the parts of the story?

A Read and listen. 🔊 8

How to Make Yarn Art

Step 1: Get ready

What's this? It's yarn art. You can make yarn art. You need a paper plate, a pencil, glue, crayons, yarn, and a paper clip.

Step 2: Make

Draw a picture on your plate. Draw an animal with your pencil. Put yarn on your animal with glue. Color your plate with crayons. Write your name.

Step 3: Hang

Put a paper clip at the top of the plate. Hang your picture on the wall or in the window.

B Look at the title. What is the topic of the text? Choose ✔ or ✘.

1. Making art with crayons ☐✔ ☒

2. Making art with yarn ✔ ✘

3. Drawing animals ✔ ✘

C Look at the headings. What do they show? Choose ✔ or ✘.

1. What you will need for each step   ✔   ⊗
2. The steps to make art   ✔   ✘
3. Animals to make   ✔   ✘

D Choose the correct answer.

1. What do you need?	(glue)	pens
2. What do you color the plate with?	colored pencils	crayons
3. When do you make the picture?	Step 1	Step 2
4. What do you draw on the plate?	a place	an animal
5. What do you put at the top of the plate?	a paper clip	yarn
6. Where can you hang the plate?	on the wall	on the door

E Complete the sentences. You will not use every word.

glue	paper clip	window	~~picture~~
calendar	clock	yarn	pencil sharpener

1. Make a ___picture___ of an animal on a paper plate.

2. Put _____ on the animal.

3. Put _____ on the yarn.

4. After you color the picture, put a _____ at the top.

5. Hang the picture in a _____

6. The pencil doesn't write. She needs a _____

Get Ready to Write

WRITING GOAL: Write a Conversation

A conversation is a talk with two or more people.
Conversations have questions and answers.

A Read the conversation. Underline the names.

Writing Tip
Names show who is speaking in a conversation. Names start with capital letters.

Sue: Why do you like art?

Ben: It makes me happy.

Sue: What kind of art do you make?

Ben: I make pictures with yarn.

B Look at **A**. What does Ben say? Complete the diagram.

Ben's Art

How he feels	What he makes
1. ___happy___	2. _____

Write

C   Think about your own art. Describe it. Complete the diagram.

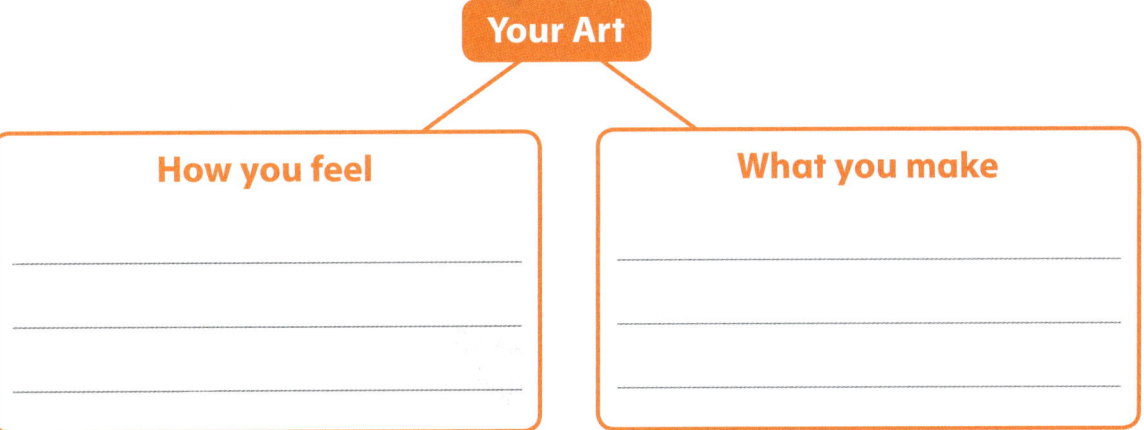

Your Art

How you feel

_____

_____

_____

What you make

_____

_____

_____

D   Now write a conversation. Use your words from **C**. Choose new words and a name, too. Then draw your favorite art project.

Sue: Why do you like art?

_____ : It makes me _____

Sue: What kind of art do you make?

_____ : _____

_____

_____

Now write a conversation about another art project you made.

MY WRITING GOAL

☐   I can write a conversation.

My Shopping Trip

MY GOALS

UNIT 3

- Read the text *Window Shopping*
- Find key information

UNIT 4

- Read the story *At the Mall*
- Find the setting

WRITE

- Write an e-mail

 A Look at the picture. What do you see?

1. What are the children doing?
2. What do the children want? What do you want in the picture?

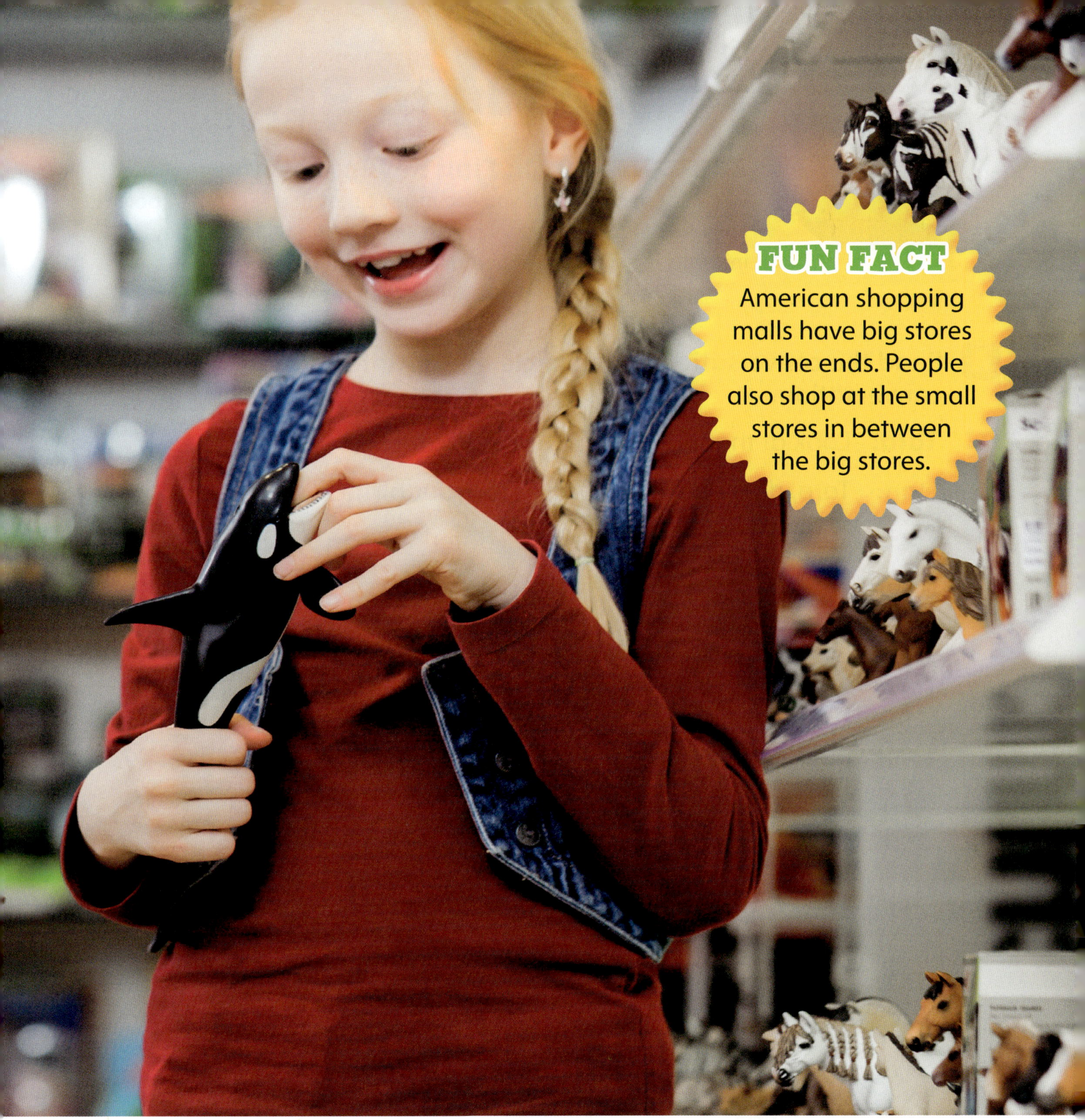

FUN FACT

American shopping malls have big stores on the ends. People also shop at the small stores in between the big stores.

B **Read the Fun Fact. Then answer the questions.**

1. Where are the small stores in American shopping malls?
2. Do you like big stores or small stores? Why?

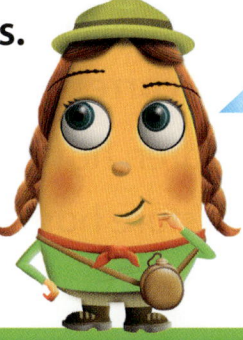

Think, Pair, Share

Where do you shop?

Get Ready to Read

READING GOAL: Find Key Information
Words or phrases that you see many times in a text are important. These words and phrases are key information. Look for key information when you read to know what a text is about.

A **Read the conversations. Then circle the key information in each conversation.**

Tara: Look at that girl, Dad. She has a (scooter)!

Dad: Tara, do you want a scooter for your birthday?

Tara: Yes! I want a scooter! A red scooter!

Later ...

Ellen: Happy birthday, Tara! What's that?

Tara: I hope it's a scooter! Let's see ... It's a red scooter. I love it!

B **Read and listen.** 🔊 9

This is **key information**.

Fun Time Toys

The Fun Time store has many toys. Do you have a yo-yo? Do you want markers for school? We sell a lot of toys! Yo-yos are $7.00. Markers are $5.00. We have every toy you want!

C **Read** **B** **again. What does the key information tell you? Choose the correct answer.**

☐ a. Children have yo-yos.

☐ b. The store has a lot of toys.

☐ c. Children want markers for school.

Read 10

What is the **key information?** Underline the sentences.

Window Shopping

Window shopping is fun! You look in a window, but you don't go in the store. You don't buy anything when you go window shopping.

Look at this window. This is a toy store. It's fun to look at toys. Look at the purple key chain. It's a small heart. Look at the orange lunch box. Now look at the comic book. Can you see a superhero?

It's fun to look in windows. Look at the pet store. Can you see a bird?

Think!

What things do you like in the windows? Do you think window shopping is fun?

Listen, point, and say.

buy

key chain

lunch box

comic book

Find the key words in the text. Then write them in your picture dictionary.

Understand

A Read *Window Shopping* again. Choose the key information.

☐ a. Comic books are funny.

☐ b. Window shopping is fun.

Remember!
Key information tells you what the text is about.

B Choose the correct answer.

1. The key chain is **small** / **big**.

2. The lunch box is **purple** / **orange**.

3. The comic book is in the **pet** / **toy** store.

C Complete the sentences.

buy	comic book	key chain	~~lunch box~~

1.

There is a ___lunch box___ in the toy store.

2.

You don't _____ things when you window shop.

3.

There is a superhero on the _____

4.

There is a purple _____ in the store.

D Read *Window Shopping* again. Work with a partner. What can you see in the toy store window? Choose **Yes** or **No**.

	Yes	No
1. key chain	✔	
2. lunch box		
3. bird		
4. superhero		

E Look at **D**. Write questions. Use *can*.

1.

Can you see a key chain?

Yes, I can.

2.

_____

Yes, I can.

3.

_____

No, I can't.

4.

_____

Yes, I can.

MY READING GOALS

☐ I can read the text.

☐ I can find key information to know what a text is about.

Get Ready to Read

READING GOAL: Find the Setting

The setting is a place in a story. When you read, ask, *Where is this?*

A Look at the pictures. Circle the settings.

1.

a store /(a school)

2.

a house / a hospital

3.

a pet store / a toy store

B Read and listen. 🔊 12

This is the **setting**.

A Fun Saturday

Eva and Marcos have a fun day. They are at a market. They look at the toys. Eva buys a toy. Marcos buys a toy, too.

C Read **B** again. Where are Marcos and Eva? Choose ✔ or ✘.

1. Marcos is at a market.   ✔ ✘

2. Eva is at school.   ✔ ✘

3. Eva is at a market.   ✔ ✘

Read 🔊 13

What is the **setting**? Underline it.

At the Mall

Woo-Jin is at the mall. "What can I buy for my dad?" he thinks. He sees an action figure. His dad doesn't like action figures. He sees a purple watch. His dad has a blue watch. Woo-Jin sees a brown wallet. His dad has a black wallet. He sees a candy bar. He buys two candy bars. He gives one candy bar to his dad. He eats the other candy bar. Gulp! Yum!

Think!

Why does Woo-Jin buy something for his dad?

Listen, point, and say.

action figure

watch

wallet

candy bar

Find the key words in the story. Then write them in your picture dictionary.

Understand

Remember!
The **setting** is where the story happens.

A Read *At the Mall* again. Where is Woo-Jin? Choose **Yes** or **No**.

1. Woo-Jin and his dad are at home.   **Yes**   (**No**)
2. Woo-Jin and his dad are in a mall.   **Yes**   **No**
3. The dad likes action figures.   **Yes**   **No**

B Choose the correct answer.

1. What color is the dad's watch?
   - [ ] a. purple
   - [✔] b. blue
2. What does Woo-Jin see?
   - [ ] a. a brown wallet
   - [ ] b. a black wallet
3. Why doesn't Woo-Jin buy his dad a wallet?
   - [ ] a. His dad has a wallet.
   - [ ] b. His dad doesn't like wallets.
4. What does Woo-Jin buy?
   - [ ] a. two candy bars
   - [ ] b. an action figure

C Complete the sentences with key words. Then match.

1. Woo-Jin's dad has a black _____ wallet.
2. Woo-Jin's dad doesn't like _____
3. Woo-Jin sees a purple _____
4. Woo-Jin eats a _____

a.    b.    c.    d.

_____   _____   __1__   _____

D Read *At the Mall* again. What does Woo-Jin see? What does his dad have? Work with a partner. Complete the table.

Woo-Jin sees ...	His dad has ...
1. a purple ____watch____	3. a blue _____
2. a brown _____	4. a black _____

E Look at **D**. Write sentences about Woo-Jin and his dad.

1.

Woo-Jin sees a purple watch.
_____

2.

_____
_____

3.

_____
_____

4.

_____
_____

MY READING GOALS

☐ I can read the story.

☐ I can find the setting and say where a story happens.

Reading Check

Remember!
Find **key information.** What information do you see many times? Find the **setting.** Where does the story happen?

A Read and listen. 🔊 15

Hello Su-Bin,

I'm at the market with my mom. I want to buy something! I see action figures and comic books. I see lunch boxes, key chains, and watches, too. I have a big lunch box and an orange watch at home. I don't need a key chain. I have $10.00 in my wallet. What can I buy?

I want to buy something for you! Look at the photo. Do you have this comic book? Do you like it?

Your friend,

Lisa

B Read the e-mail again. Is this key information? Choose ✔ or ✘.

1. Lisa doesn't have money.

2. Lisa wants to buy something.

3. Lisa sees an action figure.

C **Find the setting. Where is Lisa? Choose ✔ or ✘.**

1. She's at home.   ✔   ⊗

2. She's in a toy store.   ✔   ✘

3. She's at a market.   ✔   ✘

D **Choose the correct answer.**

1. Lisa writes an e-mail to _____
   - ✔ a. her friend.
   - ☐ b. her dad.

2. Lisa has a lunch box and _____
   - ☐ a. a watch.
   - ☐ b. a key chain.

3. Lisa sends Su-Bin _____
   - ☐ a. a wallet.
   - ☐ b. a photo.

4. Lisa wants to buy _____
   - ☐ a. a comic book.
   - ☐ b. a lunch box.

E **Unscramble and match.**

1. h l c u n   x o b
       lunch box   • Lisa doesn't need one.

2. h c a w t
                                 • Lisa has a big one at home.

3. e k y   h n i c a
                                 • Lisa sends Su-Bin a photo of this.

4. t a l w l e
                                 • Lisa has $10.00 in this.

5. m c i c o   b o k o
                                 • Lisa has an orange one.

Get Ready to Write

WRITING GOAL: Write an E-mail

An e-mail is a letter you send using the Internet. You can write about what you're doing and where you are.

A Read the e-mail. Underline the subject.

Writing Tip
Choose a word or phrase that describes your e-mail. Write it in the subject line.

TO: Joel

FROM: Ed

SUBJECT: Toys

Hi Joel,

How are you? I'm at the toy store with my mom. The store has a lot of action figures. I want to buy this one. Do you like it?

Write soon,

Ed

B Look at **A**. Complete the table.

1. **To:** Joel	2. **From:**
3. **Subject:**	4. **Where is Ed?**
5. **What does he want to buy?**	

Write

C You want to buy something at a store. Think of a friend to write to. Complete the table.

To:	From:
Subject:	**Where are you?**
What do you want to buy?	

D Now write an e-mail. Use your words from **C**. Choose new words, too. Then draw what you want to buy.

TO: _____   FROM: _____

SUBJECT: _____

Hi _____,

How are you? Today is a fun day because I'm

at _____ with _____. _____
      place   person   place

has a lot of _____. I want to buy this
              toys or things

_____. Do you like it?
  thing

_____,
  ending

_____
  your name

Now write an e-mail about a different thing to buy.

MY WRITING GOAL

☐ I can write an e-mail.

TOPIC
3
HEALTH

Fun and Games

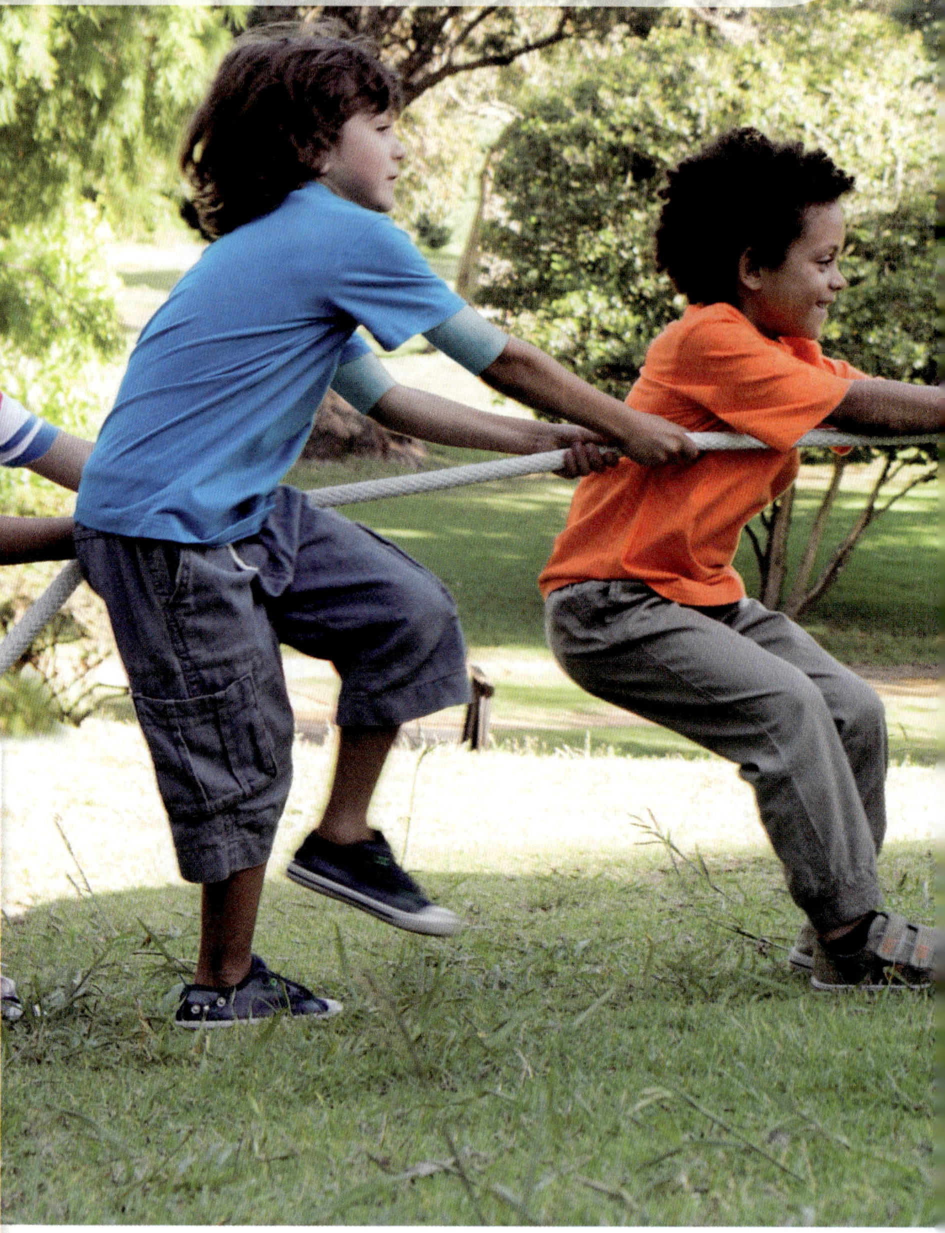

MY GOALS

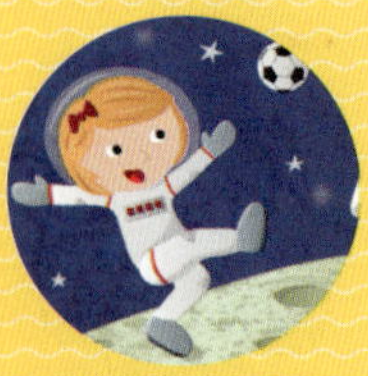

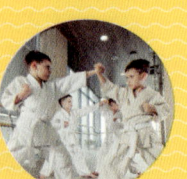

UNIT 5

- Read the story *Fun in Space*
- Find the action words

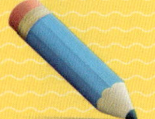

UNIT 6

- Read the poster *PlayTime*
- Find the main idea

WRITE

- Write a story

A **Look at the picture. What do you see?**

1. Where are the children?
2. Where do you play? When?

FUN FACT

Rope pulling is a very old game. It's about 4,000 years old. Today, young and old people play it everywhere.

B **Read the Fun Fact. Then answer the questions.**

1. Is rope pulling a new or old game?
2. Do you like rope pulling? What games do you like?

Think, Pair, Share
What games do you play?

Get Ready to Read

READING GOAL: Find the Action Words
Words like *swim*, *run*, and *jump* are action words. When you read, look for action words to know what the people in a story are doing.

A **Look at the pictures and read the sentences. Circle the actions.**

1.

They (play).

2.

They run.

3.

She jumps.

B **Read and listen.** 🔊 16

These are **action words**.

Kate plays at school. She plays soccer with her friends. She runs and kicks the ball. Her friends run and kick the ball, too. They play soccer every day after lunch.

C **Read** **B** **again. What does Kate do? Choose the correct answer.**

☐ a. She plays soccer and kicks the ball.

☐ b. She buys a ball at a toy store.

☐ c. She plays a video game with her friends.

Read 17

What are the **action words**? Underline them.

Fun in Space

Sophia and Dan are in space. It's time for exercise! There's no water, but they can swim. They swim in space. They move their arms and legs. Then they dance. Whee! It's fun! They want to skip. But they can't skip in spacesuits. Then they sing. "La la la la la la!" They want to play soccer. Sophia kicks the ball. Exercise in space is fun! Wait … where is the ball? Now they can't play soccer.

Think!

Do you exercise? What kind of exercises do you do?

Key Words 🔊 18

Listen, point, and say.

swim

dance

skip

sing

Find the key words in the story. Then write them in your picture dictionary.

Understand

A Read *Fun in Space* again. What do Sophia and Dan do?

☐ a. They skip in their spacesuits.

☐ b. They sing in space.

Remember!
Action words show what people are doing.

B Choose the correct answer.

1. Dan and Sophia swim in the **water /(air**).

2. They move their **arms and legs / eyes and ears**.

3. **Sophia / Dan** kicks the ball.

C Complete the sentences.

dance	sing	~~skip~~	swim

1.

Sofia and Dan don't

_____skip_____ in space.

2.

Sofia and Dan _____

in space.

3.

They _____ in space.

4.

They _____ songs

in space.

D Work with a partner. Read *Fun in Space* again. What can Sophia and Dan do in space? Complete the table.

They can …	They can't …
1. ___swim___	4. _____
2. _____	5. _____
3. _____	

E Look at **D**. What can Sophia and Dan do in space? Write. Use *can* or *can't*.

1.

_____ They can dance. _____

2.

_____

3.

_____

4.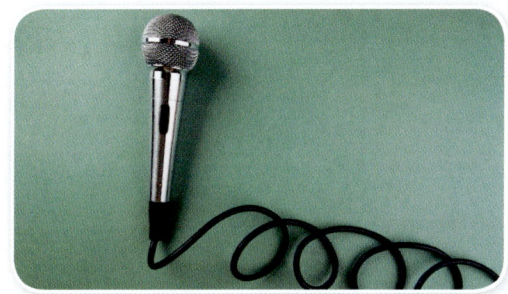

_____

MY READING GOALS

☐ I can read the story.   ☐ I can find the action words and use them to understand what people are doing.

Get Ready to Read

READING GOAL: Find the Main Idea
The main idea gives more information about the topic. You can find the main idea in the first sentence.

A Look at the pictures. Is the topic correct for each one? Choose ✔ or ✘.

1.
Topic: Art

2.
Topic: Soccer

3.
Topic: A market

B Read and listen. 🔊 19

This is the **main idea**.

You can do it!
You can exercise in many ways. You can swim in a pool. You can jump rope with friends. You can play soccer. Exercise is good for you. Exercise is fun, too!

C Read **B** again. What does the main idea tell you? Choose ✔ or ✘.

1. Swimming is the best exercise.

2. You can do different things to exercise.

3. Exercise is bad for people.

4. Exercise is fun.

Read 🔊 20

What's the **main idea**? Underline it.

PlayTime

You can do many fun things after school at PlayTime. PlayTime is three times a week for two hours.

- We jump rope on the playground on Mondays. You can play hopscotch, too.
- We do karate in the gym on Wednesdays. Mrs. Davis is a great karate teacher!
- Fridays are fun! You can ride a bike in the park with Ms. Flores, or you can ride a bike around the school with Mr. Jones.

PlayTime is great! Play with us!

Think!

What do you do after school? Do you like to do the activities at PlayTime?

Key Words 🔊 21

Listen, point, and say.

jump rope

play hopscotch

do karate

ride a bike

Find the key words in the poster. Then write them in your picture dictionary.

Understand

Remember! The **main idea** gives more information about the topic.

A Read *PlayTime* again. What does the main idea tell you? Choose **Yes** or **No**.

1. You can have fun after school. **Yes** **No**
2. You can play games in gym class. **Yes** **No**

B Choose the correct answer.

1. When do children go to PlayTime?

   ☐ a. before school ✔ b. after school

2. How many days a week is PlayTime?

   ☐ a. two ☐ b. three

3. Who teaches karate?

   ☐ a. Mrs. Davis ☐ b. Mr. Jones

4. When can you ride a bike in the park?

   ☐ a. on Wednesdays ☐ b. on Fridays

C Complete the sentences with key words. Then match.

1. You can ___jump___ rope on the playground on Monday.

2. You can _____ hopscotch on Monday, too.

3. You can _____ karate with Mrs. Davis on Wednesday.

4. You can _____ a bike in the park or around the school on Friday.

a.

b.

c.

1

d.

_____

D Work with a partner. Read *PlayTime* again. What activities can you do each day? Complete the diagram.

Monday	Wednesday	Friday
You can …	**You can …**	**You can …**
1. ___jump rope___	3. _____	4. _____
2. _____		

E Look at **D**. Write. Use *you can* and *on*.

1.

You can jump rope on Monday.
_____

2.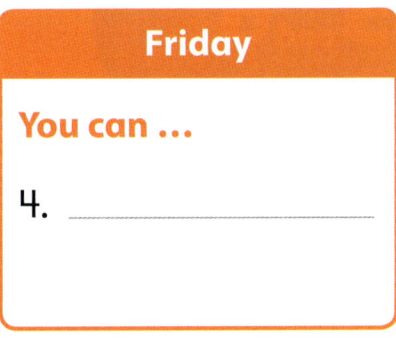

_____
_____

3.

_____
_____

4.

_____
_____

MY READING GOALS

☐ I can read a poster.

☐ I can find the main idea and use it to learn more about the topic.

Reading Check

Remember!
Find the **action words**. What are the people doing? Find the **main idea**. What does it say about the topic?

A Read and listen. 22

Let's Play!

Vicky and Ted play after school every day. They play hopscotch on Monday. They sing on Tuesday. They swim on Wednesday. They do karate on Thursday.

Today is Friday. Vicky says, "Let's dance!"

"No way!" Ted says. "Let's jump rope."

Vicky says, "No way!"

What can they do?

They see their friend Lin. She rides her bike and says, "Hello."

"I want to ride my bike with Lin!" says Vicky. "Me too!" says Ted.

B Look at the action words in the story. What do Vicky and Ted do? Choose ✔ or ✘.

1. They play hopscotch.

2. They swim.

3. They dance.

C Find the main idea. What is it? Choose ✔ or ✘.

1. Vicky and Ted sing on Tuesday. ☑✔ ⊗

2. Vicky and Ted play after school every day. ☑✔ ☐✘

3. Vicky and Ted see their friend Lin. ☑✔ ☐✘

4. Vicky and Ted want to ride their bikes. ☑✔ ☐✘

D Choose the correct answer.

1. What day is today?	**Monday**	**(Friday)**
2. When do Vicky and Ted play?	**before school**	**after school**
3. Who wants to dance?	**Vicky**	**Ted**
4. Who wants to jump rope?	**Vicky**	**Ted**
5. Who is Lin?	**their sister**	**their friend**
6. What does Lin say?	**"Hello."**	**"Me too!"**

E Complete the sentences.

dance	jump rope	play soccer	skip
do karate	~~play hopscotch~~	sing	swim

1. Vicky and Ted ___play hopscotch___ on Monday.

2. They _____ on Tuesday.

3. They _____ on Wednesday.

4. They _____ on Thursday.

5. Vicky wants to _____ on Friday.

6. Ted wants to _____ on Friday.

Get Ready to Write

WRITING GOAL: Write a Story

A story has characters and a setting, but it doesn't always happen in real life. A story can be about anything.

A **Read the story. Who are the characters? What is the setting?**

Writing Tip
When you write a story, choose a character and a setting.

Cara plays in a pool all day. She swims, dances, and does karate in the water. She says, "Kiai!"
Pedro runs to the water. He says, "Oh, no!" But Cara is OK.
"Oh, karate!" Pedro says. He jumps into the water. He does karate with Cara.

Kiai!

B **Look at** **A**. **Complete the diagram with the setting, characters, and actions.**

Setting

1. _____

Character 1

2. _____

4. _____ swims _____

_____

_____

Character 2

3. _____

5. runs to the water

_____

_____

Write

C Think about the setting, characters, and actions for a story. Complete the diagram.

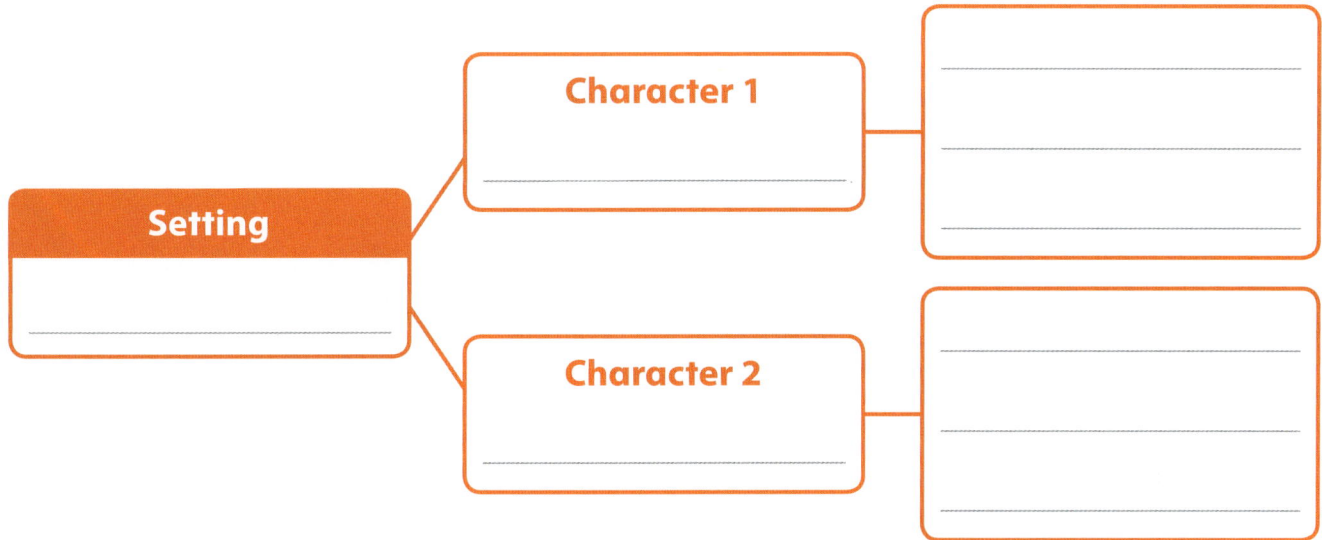

	Character 1	
Setting		
	Character 2	

D Now write a story. Use your words from **A**. Choose new words, too. Then draw a picture for your story.

_____ is in _____. _____
 name   place   he/she

_____.
         actions

_____ _____.
 name/he/she   actions

_____ _____.
 name/he/she   actions

_____ _____.
 name/he/she   actions

Now write a story with a different setting and different characters.

MY WRITING GOAL

☐ I can write a story.

My Heroes

MY GOALS

UNIT 7

- Read the text *Great Jobs*
- Find the places

UNIT 8

- Read the story *Hero for a Day*
- Understand cause and effect

WRITE

- Write a paragraph

 A **Look at the picture. What do you see?**

1. How many people do you see? Who are they?

2. How does the child feel about his mom and dad?

FUN FACT

The word *hero* comes from the Greek language. Many children think their moms, dads, and teachers are heroes.

B Read the Fun Fact. Then answer the questions.

1. Is the word *hero* old or new?

2. Why do you think moms, dads, and teachers are heroes?

Think, Pair, Share
Who are your heroes? Why?

Get Ready to Read

READING GOAL: Find the Places

Places are countries, cities, and buildings, like *South Korea*, *New York City*, and *schools*. Find places in a text to understand where people are.

A **Look at the pictures. Circle the places.**

1.

(a restaurant) /
a playground

2.

a house /
Tokyo, Japan

3.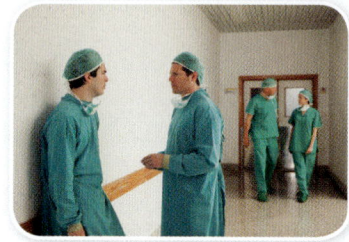

a school / a hospital

B **Read and listen.** 🔊 23

These are **places**.

My heroes are my mom and dad.
My mom is an art teacher. She works in
a school. My dad makes food in a restaurant.
We live in a nice house in Greenville in
the United States.

C **Read B again. Which place in the text is a city? Choose the correct answer.**

☐ a. restaurant

☐ b. Greenville

☐ c. the United States

Read  24

What **places** are in the text? Underline them.

Listen, point, and say.

cook

dentist

doctor

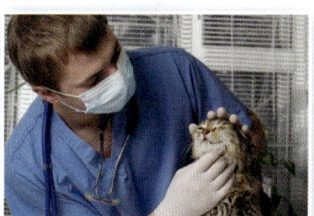

vet

www.jobcorner.osw/greatjobs

Great Jobs

What are some great jobs?

Paul   My dad works in a cool restaurant! He's a cook. I want to be a cook in Japan one day!

Tim   My mom cleans and fixes teeth. She's a dentist in Miami. She loves her job!

Sandra   Doctors help sick people in hospitals around the world. My dad is a doctor. He's great!

Eva   A vet is my hero! Dr. Brown helps my cat. She's a good vet.

Find the key words in the text. Then write them in your picture dictionary.

Think!

Which jobs do you think are great? Which job do you want?

Understand

A Read *Great Jobs* again. Which buildings are in the text?

☐ a. hospital and restaurant

☐ b. restaurant and school

Remember!
Places in a text help us understand where the people are.

B Choose the correct answer.

1. Tim's (mom) / **dad** is a dentist.

2. Paul wants to work in a **hospital / restaurant**.

3. Eva's hero is a **doctor / vet**.

C Complete the sentences.

| ~~cook~~ | dentist | doctor | vet |

1.

A ___cook___ works in a restaurant.

2.

A _____ works in an animal hospital.

3.

A _____ works in a hospital.

4.

A _____ works in an office.

D Work with a partner. Read *Great Jobs* again. What jobs are in the text? Complete the diagram.

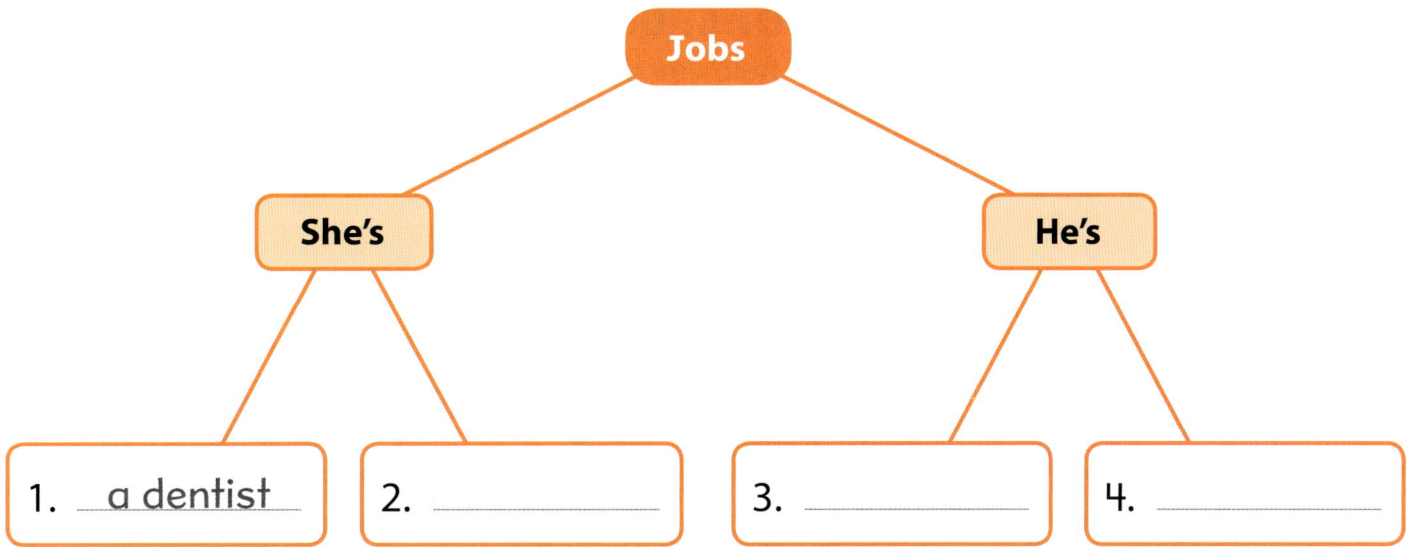

Jobs

She's

He's

1. a dentist

2. _____

3. _____

4. _____

E Look at **D**. Write about the jobs. Use *he's* or *she's*.

1.

She's a dentist.

2.

_____

3.

_____

4.

_____

MY READING GOALS

☐ I can read the text.

☐ I can find places and use them to understand where people are.

Get Ready to Read

READING GOAL: Understand Cause and Effect

Cause and effect help you understand why things happen in a text. The cause is *why* something happens. And the effect is what happens *after*.

A Look at the cause. Circle the effect.

Cause

Effect

B Read and listen. 🔊 26

This is **cause** and **effect**.

Don is a cook. He is in his restaurant.

Oops! He hurts his tooth. Ouch!

He goes to the dentist. Dr. Wang fixes his tooth.

C Read **B** again. Why does Don go to the dentist? Choose ✔ or ✘.

1. He falls at work.   ✔   ⊗

2. His teeth aren't clean.   ✔   ✘

3. He hurts his tooth.   ✔   ✘

Read 27

Look at the underlined **causes**. What are the **effects**? Circle them.

Hero for a Day

A cat sees a bird in a tree. The cat runs up the tree.

A soccer player is in a taxi. She sees the cat.

"Stop!" she says. "That's my cat!" The taxi driver stops.

The soccer player gets out of the taxi.

She says, "Help!" A police officer runs to the tree.

"Come down!" the police officer says to the cat.

The cat doesn't move.

A firefighter climbs the tree. She gets the cat.

The soccer player says, "Thank you." The firefighter says, "You're welcome." The cat says, "Meow."

Key Words  28

Listen, point, and say.

soccer player

taxi driver

police officer

firefighter

Find the key words in the story. Then write them in your picture dictionary.

Think!

Who is the hero of the story? Why?

Understand

Remember!
A **cause** is *why* something happens. An **effect** is what happens *after* the cause.

A Read *Hero for a Day* again. What happens after the soccer player says "Thank you"? Choose **Yes** or **No.**

1. The cat says, "Meow."   **Yes**   **No**
2. The firefighter says, "You're welcome."   **Yes**   **No**

B Choose the correct answer.

1. Who is in the taxi?
   - ☑ a. a soccer player
   - ☐ b. a police officer
2. What does the soccer player see?
   - ☐ a. a bird in the air
   - ☐ b. a cat in a tree
3. Who says, "Come down"?
   - ☐ a. the soccer player
   - ☐ b. the police officer

C Complete the sentences with key words. Then match.

1. The ___police officer___ runs to the tree.
2. The _____ stops the car.
3. The _____ gets the cat.
4. The _____ sees her cat.

a.

b.

c.

1

d.

_____   _____   _____   _____

D Work with a partner. What are the causes and effects in the story? Complete the table.

Cause		Effect
1. A ____cat____ sees a bird in a tree.	→	The _____ runs up the tree.
2. The _____ says, "Stop!"	→	The _____ stops.
3. The _____ says, "Help!"	→	A _____ runs to the tree.
4. A _____ climbs the tree.	→	She gets the _____

E Look at **D**. Write. Combine the cause and effect with *because*.

1. The cat runs up the tree ___because___ it
   sees a bird in the tree.

2. The taxi driver stops _____ the soccer player
   _____

3. The police officer runs to the tree _____ the soccer player
   _____

4. The firefighter gets the cat _____ she
   _____

MY READING GOALS

☐ I can read the story.   ☐ I can understand cause and effect, and use it to understand why things happen.

Reading Check

Remember!
Find the **places**. Where are the people? Understand **cause** and **effect**. Why do things happen?

A Read and listen.  29

My Hero
by Luke Smith

Who is your hero? A firefighter? A police officer? A cook? A doctor?

My hero is my mom! She's a vet. She's a dentist, too. She's a dentist for pets! She works in an animal hospital. She works on farms, too. She cleans cats' teeth. She cleans horses' teeth, too. She helps animals because they have problems with their teeth. People love their pets. My mom is their hero, too.

B Look at the places in the text. Where does Luke's mom work? Choose ✔ or ✘.

1. on farms

2. in a restaurant

3. in an animal hospital

C Look for cause and effect in the text. Why does Luke's mom help animals? Choose ✔ or ✗.

1. because they are up in trees and can't get down   ✔   ⊗

2. because they don't want to eat their food   ✔   ✗

3. because they have problems with their teeth   ✔   ✗

D Choose the correct answer.

1. Luke's hero is _____
   - ☐ a. a firefighter.
   - ☑ b. his mom.

2. Luke's mom is _____
   - ☐ a. a vet and a dentist.
   - ☐ b. a doctor and a cook.

3. Luke's mom cleans _____
   - ☐ a. houses.
   - ☐ b. teeth.

4. Luke's mom is many people's _____
   - ☐ a. hero.
   - ☐ b. dentist.

E Unscramble and match.

1. c s e c r o   a p e y r l

   _____ soccer player _____ •

    • This person drives a car for work.

2. x i t a   v d i e r r •

   _____

    • This person cleans teeth.

3. c r d t o o •

   _____

    • This person works in a hospital.

4. s n t d e t i •

   _____

    • This person kicks a ball.

Get Ready to Write

WRITING GOAL: Write a Paragraph

A paragraph is three or more sentences about the same idea. The first sentence has the main idea. The other sentences give information about the main idea.

A Read the paragraph. Underline *in* + place.

Writing Tip
Use *in* to show where things happen.

My Hero
by Rick Vargas
My hero is my dad. He's a doctor.
He works in a hospital. We play soccer
in the park on Saturdays. After soccer,
we have lunch in a restaurant.

B Look at **A**. Who is Rick's hero? Complete the diagram.

My Hero

1. _my dad_

Job

2. _____

What we do

4. _____
_____

Where

3. _____

When

5. _____

Write

C Think about your hero. Complete the diagram.

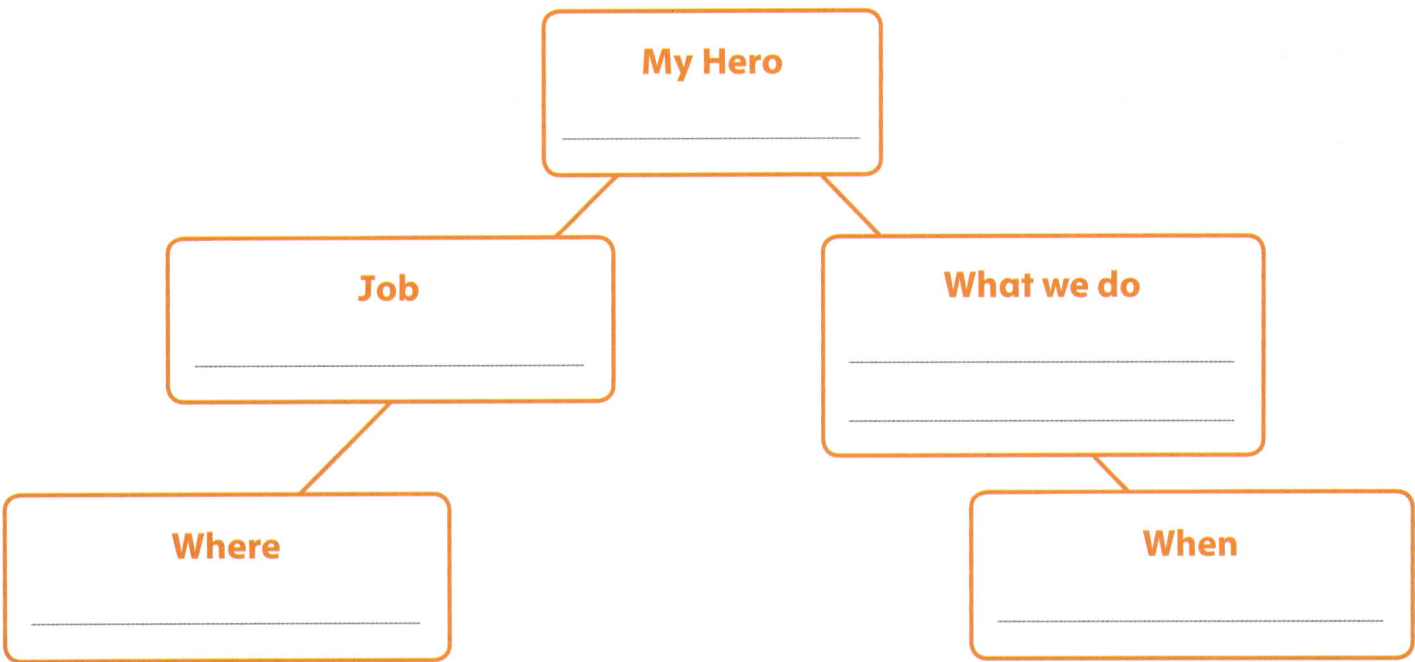

My Hero

_____

Job

_____

What we do

_____

_____

Where

_____

When

_____

D Now write a paragraph about your hero. Use your words from **C**. Choose new words, too. Then draw your hero.

My hero is _____.
                       name

_____ a _____.
  He's/She's   job

_____ works in _____.
  He/She   place

We _____.
          action

Now write a paragraph about a person with a different job.

Yum!

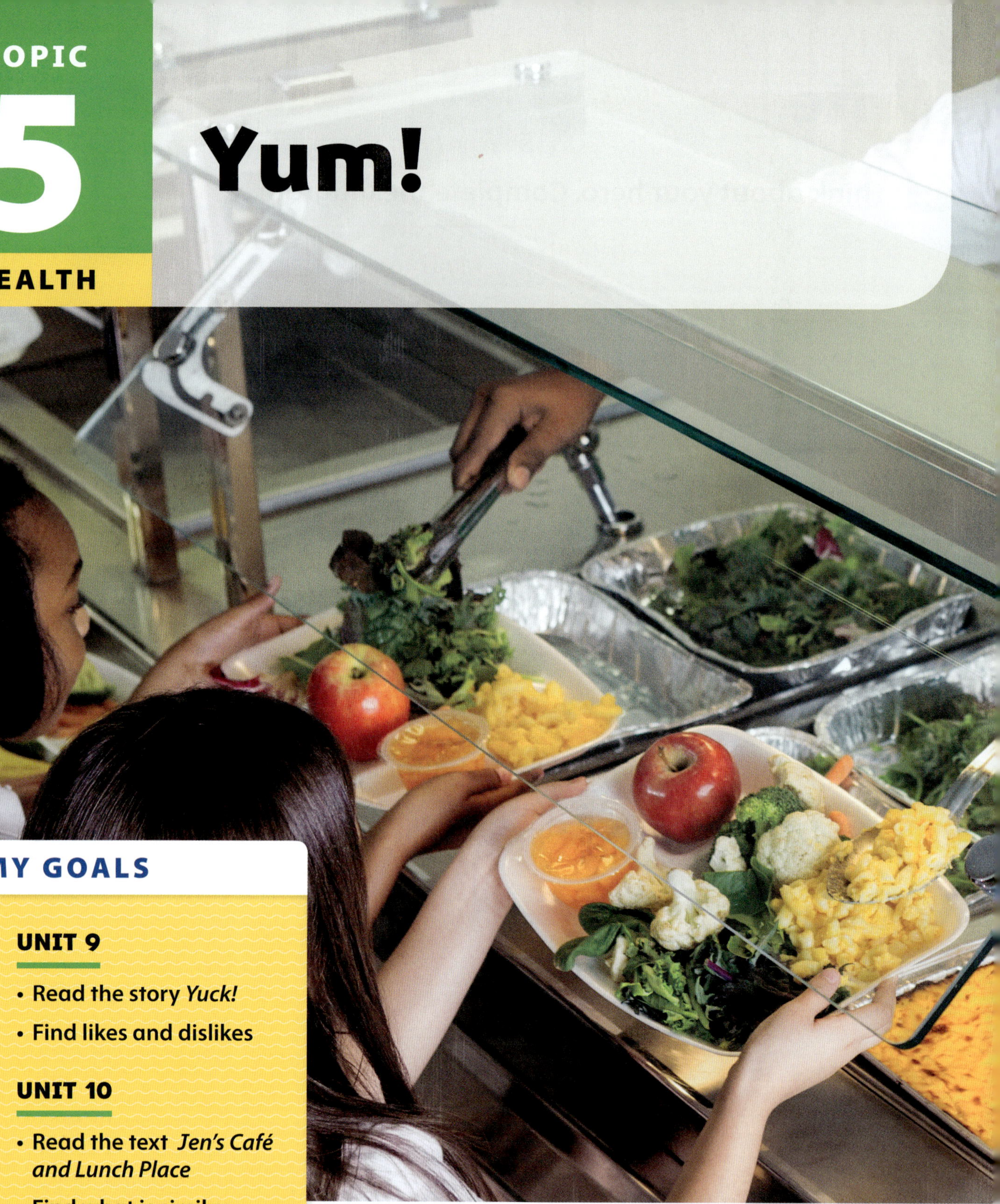

MY GOALS

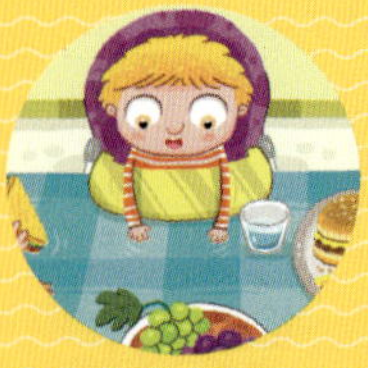

UNIT 9

- Read the story *Yuck!*
- Find likes and dislikes

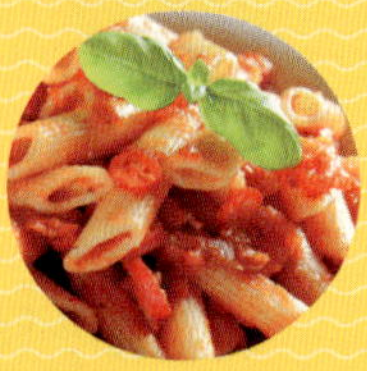

UNIT 10

- Read the text *Jen's Café and Lunch Place*
- Find what is similar and different

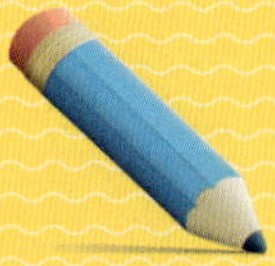

WRITE

- Write an opinion

A Look at the picture. What do you see?

1. What are the children doing?
2. Do you like their food? Why or why not?

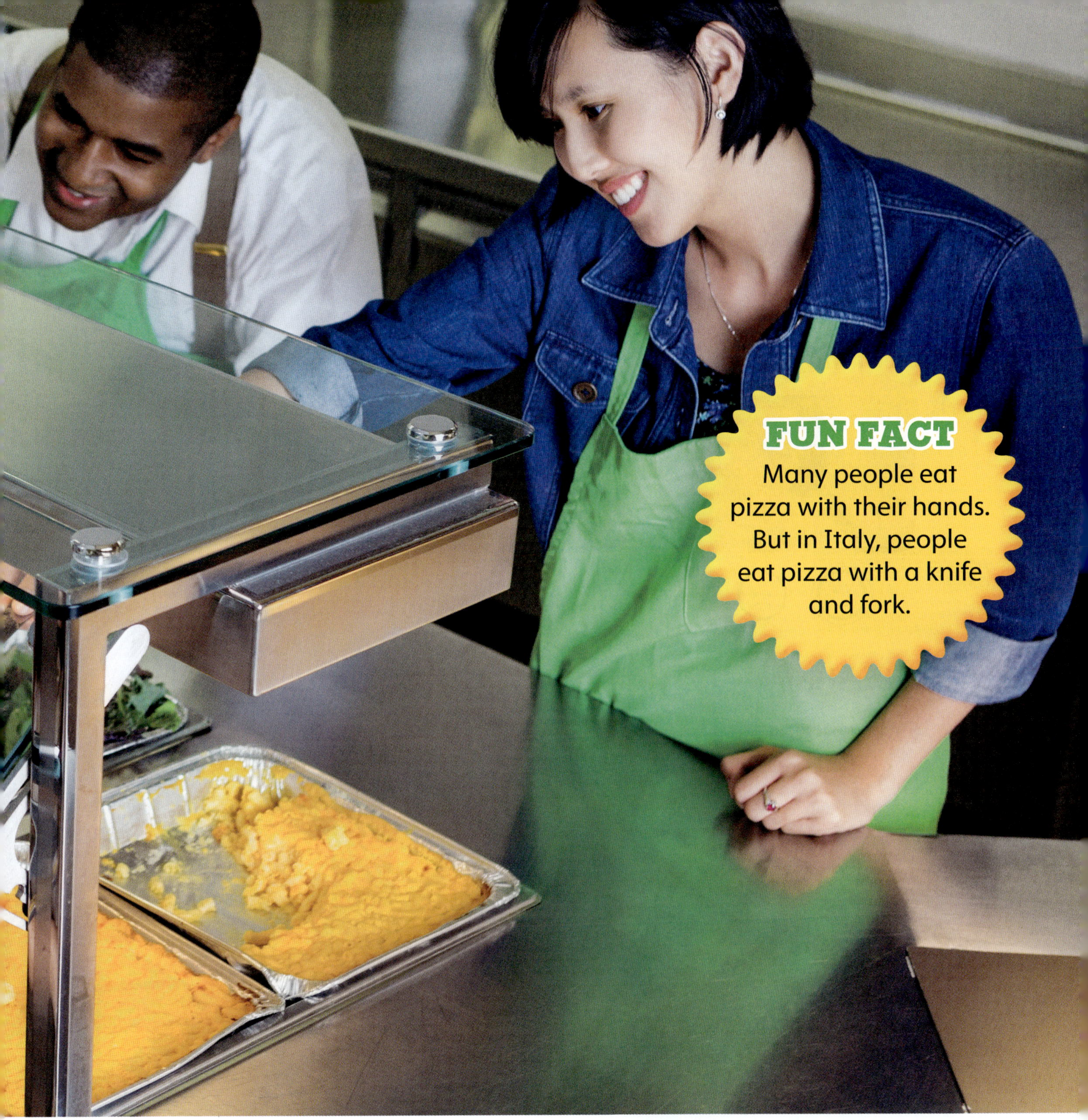

B Read the Fun Fact. Then answer the questions.

1. How do people eat pizza in Italy?

2. How do you eat pizza?

Think, Pair, Share
What do you eat with your hands?

Get Ready to Read

READING GOAL: Find Likes and Dislikes

Likes are things people think are good. *Dislikes* are things people think are bad. Find likes and dislikes in a text to understand how people feel about things.

A Look at the pictures. Circle 😊 for *likes* and 😕 for *dislikes*.

1.  2.  3.

B Read and listen. 🔊 30

These are **likes** and (dislikes).

Todd:	Look at my lunch! I like pizza.
Mia:	I like pizza, too! But I don't like juice.
Vicky:	I don't like pizza.
Mia:	Wow! Really, Vicky?
Vicky:	Really! But I like juice.

C Read **B** again. What does Mia like? Choose the correct answer.

☐ a. pizza   ☐ b. juice   ☐ c. pizza and juice

Read 31

What are the **likes** and **dislikes**? Underline the likes. Circle the dislikes.

---

www.whatkidslike.osw/max

Yuck!

Max is Toby and Linda's little brother. He can eat "big kid" food now.

"Do you want a bite of my sandwich?" Linda asks. "Yes," says Max. Then he says, "Yuck!" Max doesn't like sandwiches.

"Do you want a bite of my burger with cheese?" Toby asks. "Yes," says Max. Then he says, "Yuck." Max doesn't like burgers, and he doesn't like cheese.

"Here Max, try some grapes," Toby and Linda say. "Yum!" says Max. He likes grapes. "Yay!" say Toby and Linda.

Listen, point, and say.

sandwich

burger

cheese

grapes

Find the key words in the story. Then write them in your picture dictionary.

Think!

What foods don't you like?

Understand

A Read *Yuck!* again. What does Max like?

☐ a. cheese

☐ b. grapes

> **Remember!**
> **Likes** and **dislikes** show how people feel about things.

B Choose the correct answer.

1. Max is Linda's **friend** / (**brother**).

2. Max sees the sandwich and says, **"Yum."** / **"Yuck."**

3. Toby gives Max a bite of his **burger** / **sandwich**.

C Complete the sentences.

| burger | cheese | ~~grapes~~ | sandwich |

1.

Does Max like ___grapes?___

2.

Toby likes _____

3.

Linda has a _____

4.

Toby has a _____

D Work with a partner. What does Max like? Complete the diagram.

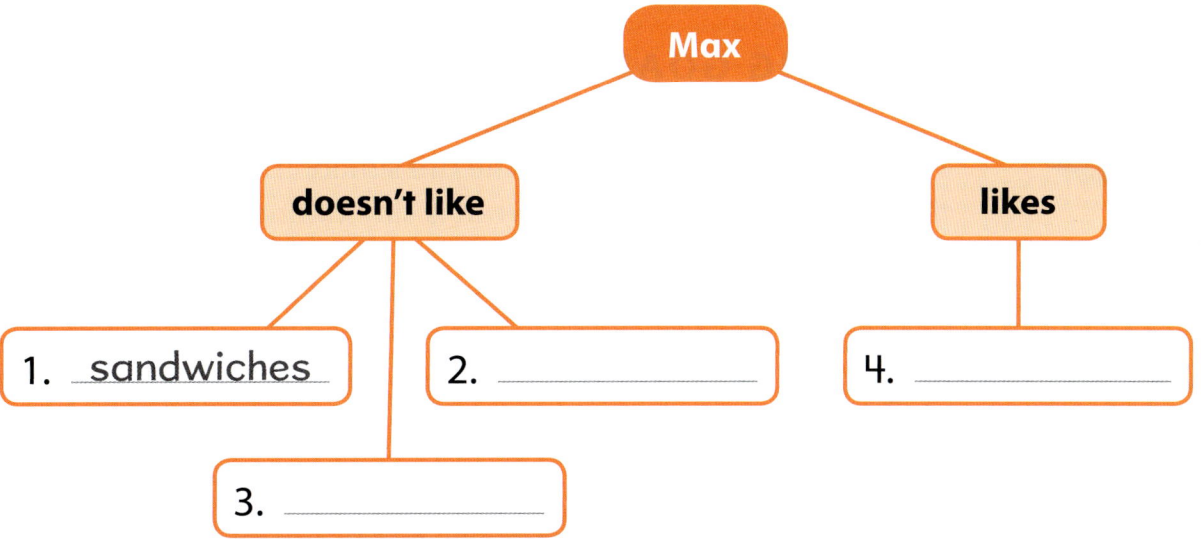

```
                        Max
           ┌─────────────┴─────────────┐
      doesn't like                   likes
     ┌─────┼─────┐                     │
  1. sandwiches  2. _____      4. _____
        │
     3. _____
```

E Look at **D**. Write sentences. Use *likes* or *doesn't like*.

1.

Max doesn't like sandwiches. _____

2.

_____

3.

_____

4.

_____

MY READING GOALS

☐ I can read a story. ☐ I can find likes and dislikes and use them to understand how people feel about things.

Get Ready to Read

READING GOAL: Find What Is Similar and Different

Things that are almost the same are similar. Things that are not the same are different. Find what is similar and what is different to learn more about a text.

A Underline the things that are similar. Circle the things that are different.

B Read and listen. 33

These things are **similar** and **different**.

Jen's Café
Today's Special: A burger with cheese, grapes, juice, and cake

Lunch Place
Today's Special: A burger with lettuce, grapes, a smoothie, and cake

C Read **B** again. How are the places similar and different? Choose ✔ or ✗.

1. The special at Jen's Café has a burger.
   The special at Lunch Place has a burger.

2. The special at Jen's Café has lettuce.
   The special at Lunch Place has cheese.

Read 34

What things are **similar**? Underline them. What things are **different**? Circle them.

Jen's Café and Lunch Place

by Josh Gardner ★★★☆☆

Jen's Café is new, but Lunch Place is old. Jen's Café is good, and Lunch Place is good, too! They both have burgers and steak. Lunch Place has stew, but Jen's Café doesn't. Both restaurants have brown rice. Jen's Café has pasta with red sauce, and Lunch Place has pasta with white sauce. Jen's Café has windows, but Lunch Place doesn't. I like Jen's Café. I can sit by the window and see the city. It's nice!

Think!

Which restaurant do you like? Why?

Key Words 35

Listen, point, and say.

steak

stew

rice

pasta

Find the key words in the text. Then write them in your picture dictionary.

Understand

A Read *Jen's Café and Lunch Place* again. How are the restaurants similar and different? Choose **Yes** or **No**.

1. They both have burgers. (Yes)   No
2. They both have stew.   Yes   No
3. The pasta is different at the restaurants.   Yes   No

B Choose the correct answer.

1. Is Jen's Café a new restaurant?
   ✔ a. Yes, it is.   ☐ b. No, it isn't.
2. What color is the sauce at Lunch Place?
   ☐ a. white   ☐ b. red
3. Where does Josh like to sit at Jen's Café?
   ☐ a. on the street   ☐ b. by the window

C Complete the sentences with key words. Then match.

1. Jen's Café has ____pasta____ with red sauce.
2. Both restaurants have brown _____.
3. Both restaurants have burgers and _____
4. Jen's place doesn't have _____

a.

b.

c.

d.

a. _____   b. _____   c. _____   d. ____1____

D Work with a partner. How are the restaurants similar and different? Complete the diagram.

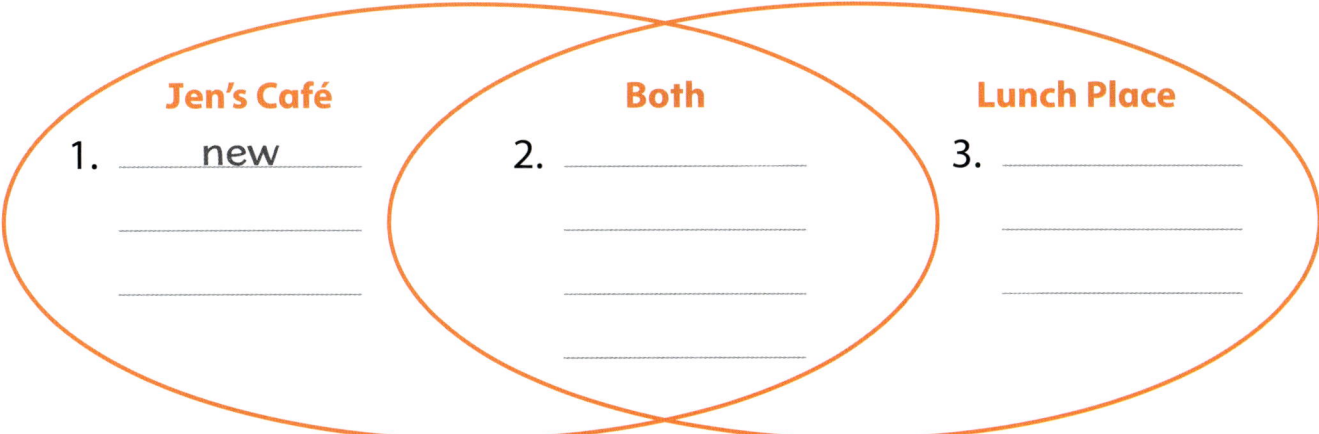

Jen's Café

1. __new__
_____
_____

Both

2. _____
_____
_____
_____

Lunch Place

3. _____
_____
_____

E Look at **D**. Write. Use *has* or *doesn't have*.

1.

Jen's Café ___has brown rice___,
and Lunch Place __has brown rice.__

2.

Jen's Café _____,
but Lunch Place _____

3.

Jen's Café _____,
and Lunch Place _____

4.

Jen's Café _____
with red sauce, but Lunch Place
_____ with white sauce.

MY READING GOALS

☐ I can read the text.   ☐ I can find things that are similar and different and use them to learn more about a text.

Remember!
Find **likes** and **dislikes**. How do people feel about things? Find things that are **similar** and **different**. What do they tell you about the text?

A Read and listen. 🔊 36

Our Favorite Foods

by Ji-Min Kim

I like a lot of foods. I like brown rice, but my brother likes white rice. We like pasta. I like pasta with red sauce, but my brother doesn't. He likes white sauce.

We both like burgers. I like burgers with cheese, but my brother doesn't like cheese.

I like sandwiches, and my brother likes them, too. I like cheese sandwiches, but my brother doesn't like them. He likes steak sandwiches.

My dad makes great stew. We both like it! What foods do you like?

B Look at likes and dislikes in the text. What does Ji-Min's brother like? Choose ✔ or ✘.

1. brown rice   ✔   ⊗

2. burgers   ✔   ✘

3. stew   ✔   ✘

C How are Ji-Min and her brother similar and different? Choose ✔ or ✘.

1. They both like rice.   ✅ ✘

2. They both like pasta.   ✔ ✘

3. They both like cheese.   ✔ ✘

D Choose the correct answer.

1. Who likes brown rice?	**(Ji-Min)**		**her brother**
2. Who likes white rice?	**Ji-Min**		**her brother**
3. Who likes pasta with red sauce?	**Ji-Min**		**her brother**
4. Who likes pasta with white sauce?	**Ji-Min**		**her brother**
5. What does her brother like?	**burgers**		**cheese**
6. What kind of sandwiches does her brother like?	**cheese**		**steak**
7. Who makes stew?	**her brother**		**her dad**

E Complete the sentences.

burger	grapes	rice	steak
cheese	~~pasta~~	sandwich	stew

1. I don't like _____pasta_____ with white sauce.

2. I like green and purple _____

3. I like white and brown _____

4. I like yellow and orange _____

5. We make _____ in a hot pan.

6. Do you want a cheese _____ or a burger for lunch?

Get Ready to Write

WRITING GOAL: Write an Opinion

An opinion shows what you think about something.
It shows if you like or dislike something.

A Read Fred's text. Underline the similar opinions.
Circle the different opinions.

> **Writing Tip**
> Use *and* to show things are similar.
> Use *but* to show things are different.

I like pizza, and my sister likes it, too.
I don't like burgers, but my sister likes
them. I like steak sandwiches, but my
sister doesn't like them. I like cheese
sandwiches, and my sister does, too.

B Look at **A**. What does Fred like? What does his sister like?
What do they both like? Complete the diagram.

Fred
1. __steak sandwiches__

Both
2. _____
_____

His Sister
3. _____

Write

C Think about food that you and a friend like. Complete the diagram.

I like   **We both like**   **My friend likes**

_____   _____   _____

_____   _____   _____

D Now write an opinion. Use your words from **C**. Choose new words, too. Then draw the food you like.

I like _____, but _____ doesn't like it.
          food   friend's name

I like _____, and _____ likes it, too.
          food   friend's name

I don't like _____, but _____ likes it.
            food   friend's name

I _____, _____
                  friend's name

_____.

I _____, _____
                  friend's name

_____.

Now write an opinion about a restaurant.

MY WRITING GOAL

☐ **I can write an opinion.**

My Day

MY GOALS

UNIT 11

- Read the text messages
- Find times

UNIT 12

- Read the story *Where, Oh Where?*
- Understand the sequence

WRITE

- Write a schedule

A Look at the picture. What do you see?

1. Where are the children? What are they doing?
2. Do you have a bed like this? What is your bed like?

FUN FACT

Babies sleep for over 15 hours a day. Kids aged 7 to 12 need about 10 hours of sleep every night.

B **Read the Fun Fact. Then answer the questions.**

1. How many hours do babies sleep?

2. How many hours do you sleep at night?

Think, Pair, Share
Do you sleep more on the weekends? Why or why not?

Get Ready to Read

READING GOAL: Find Times

Times show when things happen. For example, 7:30 a.m. and 2:00 p.m. are times. Look for times when you read.

A The pictures are in the correct order. Match the times to the pictures.

1.  c

2.

3.

   a. 11:30 a.m.   b. 12:30 p.m.   c. 11:00 a.m.

B Read and listen. 🔊 37

These are **times**.

Saturday, October 8

10:00 a.m.	Take the cat to the vet with Dad.
12:00 p.m.	Soccer game — leave at 11:30 a.m.
1:30 p.m.	Have lunch at Dino's Pizza Place with the soccer team.

C Read **B** again. What time is Sue's soccer game? Choose the correct answer.

   a. at 11:30 a.m.   b. at 12:00 p.m.   c. at 1:30 p.m.

Read 38

What **times** are in the text messages? Underline them.

Messages

Tom: Hi, Ann! Look at this photo. My brother is tired!

Ann: Funny! What time do you get up at your house?

Tom: We get up at 6:00 a.m.

Ann: Wow! That's early! I get up at 7:30 a.m. Then, we have breakfast at 8:00.

Tom: Do you brush your teeth before or after breakfast?

Ann: After, of course! About 8:15.

Tom: Me too! What time do you go to school?

Ann: At 8:30. Hey, I'm going to be late. Stop texting me!

Tom: OK. See you at school!

Listen, point, and say.

get up

have breakfast

brush your teeth

go to school

Find the key words in the text messages. Then write them in your picture dictionary.

Think!

What time do you do the things in the messages?

Understand

Remember!
Times show when things happen.

A Read the text messages again. How does the time explain why Tom's brother is tired?

☐ a. because it's early in the morning

☐ b. because it's late at night

B Choose the correct answer.

1. **Ann** /(**Tom**) sends a picture in a text message.

2. Ann brushes her teeth **before / after** breakfast.

3. Ann and Tom go to **the same school / different schools**.

C Complete the sentences.

| brushes his teeth | ~~gets up~~ | goes to school | has breakfast |

1.

Tom _____ gets up _____ at 6:00 a.m.

2.

He _____ with his brother.

3.

He _____ after breakfast.

4.

He _____ in the morning.

D Work with a partner. Read the text messages. What does Ann do in the morning? Complete the diagram.

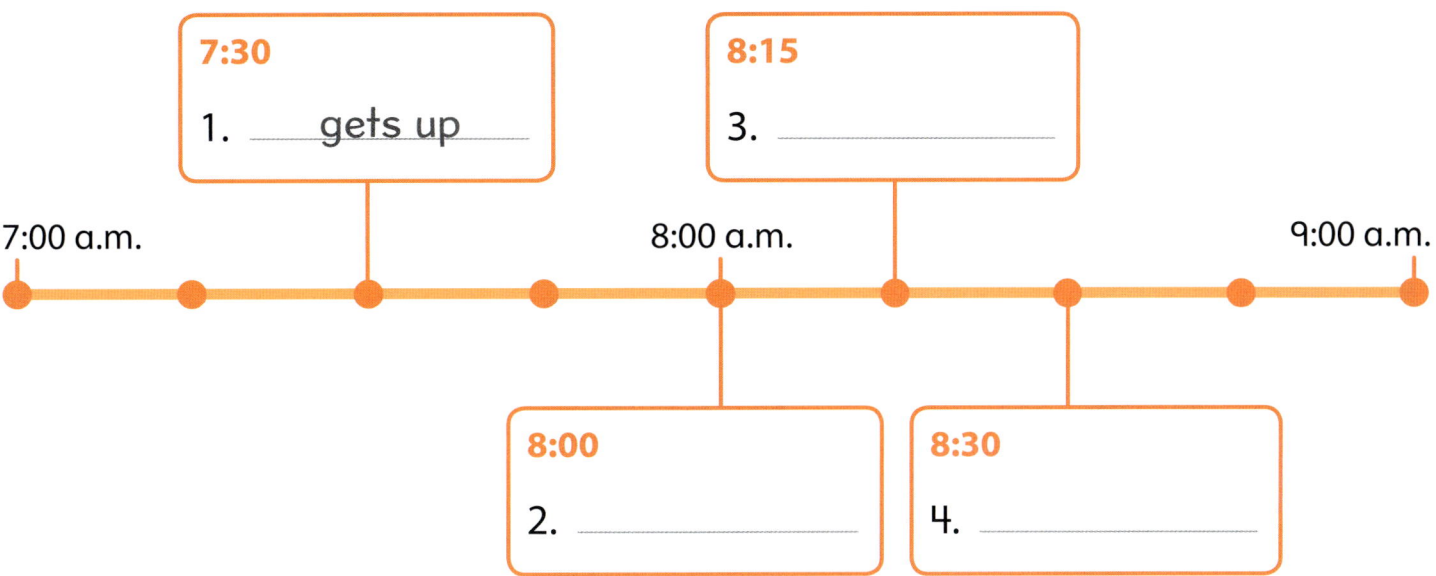

7:30

1. _____gets up_____

8:15

3. _____

7:00 a.m.   8:00 a.m.   9:00 a.m.

8:00

2. _____

8:30

4. _____

E Look at **D**. Write.

1.

_____She gets up_____ at 7:30.

2.

_____ at 8:00.

3.

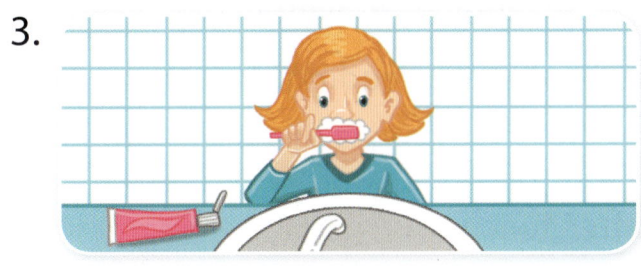

_____ at 8:15.

4.

_____ at 8:30.

MY READING GOALS

☐ I can read text messages.

☐ I can find times and use them to understand when things happen.

Get Ready to Read

READING GOAL: Understand the Sequence

The sequence is the order that things happen in a story. Words like *first, next, then,* and *finally* help you understand the sequence.

A **Read the sentences. What happens first? Order the pictures.**

Then, I brush my teeth.

Finally, I'm ready for school!

1

First, I have breakfast.

B **Read and listen.**  40

These sentences show the **sequence**.

Joe: What classes do you have at your new school?

Maria: First, we have math. Next, we have reading.

Joe: I see.

Maria: Then, we have science after lunch.
Finally, we have art at 2:00 p.m.

C **Read B again. What is the sequence of Maria's day? Choose ✔ or ✘.**

1. Math is before reading. ✓ ✘

2. Reading is after science. ✔ ✘

3. Art is last. ✔ ✘

Which sentences show the **sequence** of Ben's day? Underline them.

Where, *Oh* Where?

by Ruth Morgan

It is 5:00 p.m. Where is my brother Ben?
Ben gets home from school at 3:30 p.m. This is his usual day. First, he does homework. Then, we eat dinner. Next, he watches TV. Finally, he goes to bed.

I look for Ben. I see his homework. I don't see him. I see his dinner plate. I don't see him. I see the TV is on. But I don't see Ben.

I open his bedroom door. I find Ben! He is in bed at 5:00 p.m. He is tired today!

Think!

What do you do after school?

Key Words 🔊 42

Listen, point, and say.

do homework

eat dinner

watch TV

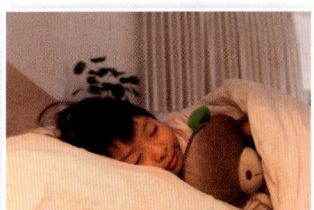

go to bed

Find the key words in the story. Then write them in your picture dictionary.

Understand

Remember!
The **sequence** is the order things happen.

A Read *Where, Oh Where?* again. Why is the sequence of Ben's day important? Choose **Yes** or **No**.

1. It helps Ruth find a good TV show.   **Yes**   (**No**)

2. It shows when Ruth eats dinner with him.   **Yes**   **No**

3. It helps Ruth know where to look for him.   **Yes**   **No**

B Choose the correct answer.

1. What time does Ben get home from school?

   ☑ a. 3:30   ☐ b. 4:00

2. When does Ben usually eat dinner?

   ☐ a. before he watches TV   ☐ b. after he watches TV

3. Where does Ruth find Ben?

   ☐ a. by the TV   ☐ b. in his bed

C Complete the sentences with key words. Then match.

1. I ___eat dinner___ at 6:30 p.m. We have chicken on Friday!

2. I _____ at my desk. Today, it's math.

3. I _____ at 8:00 p.m. I sleep in a small bed.

4. I _____ on Saturdays. I like shows about superheroes.

a.    b.    c.    d.

_____   _____   _____1_____   _____

D Work with a partner. What does Ruth do? Complete the diagram.

1 She sees Ben's homework. _____

2 She sees his _____

3 She sees the TV _____

4 She opens _____

5 She finds _____

E Look at **D**. Write. Use *before*.

1.

Ruth sees Ben's homework before she sees his dinner plate.

2.

Ruth _____

3.

Ruth _____

4.

Ruth _____

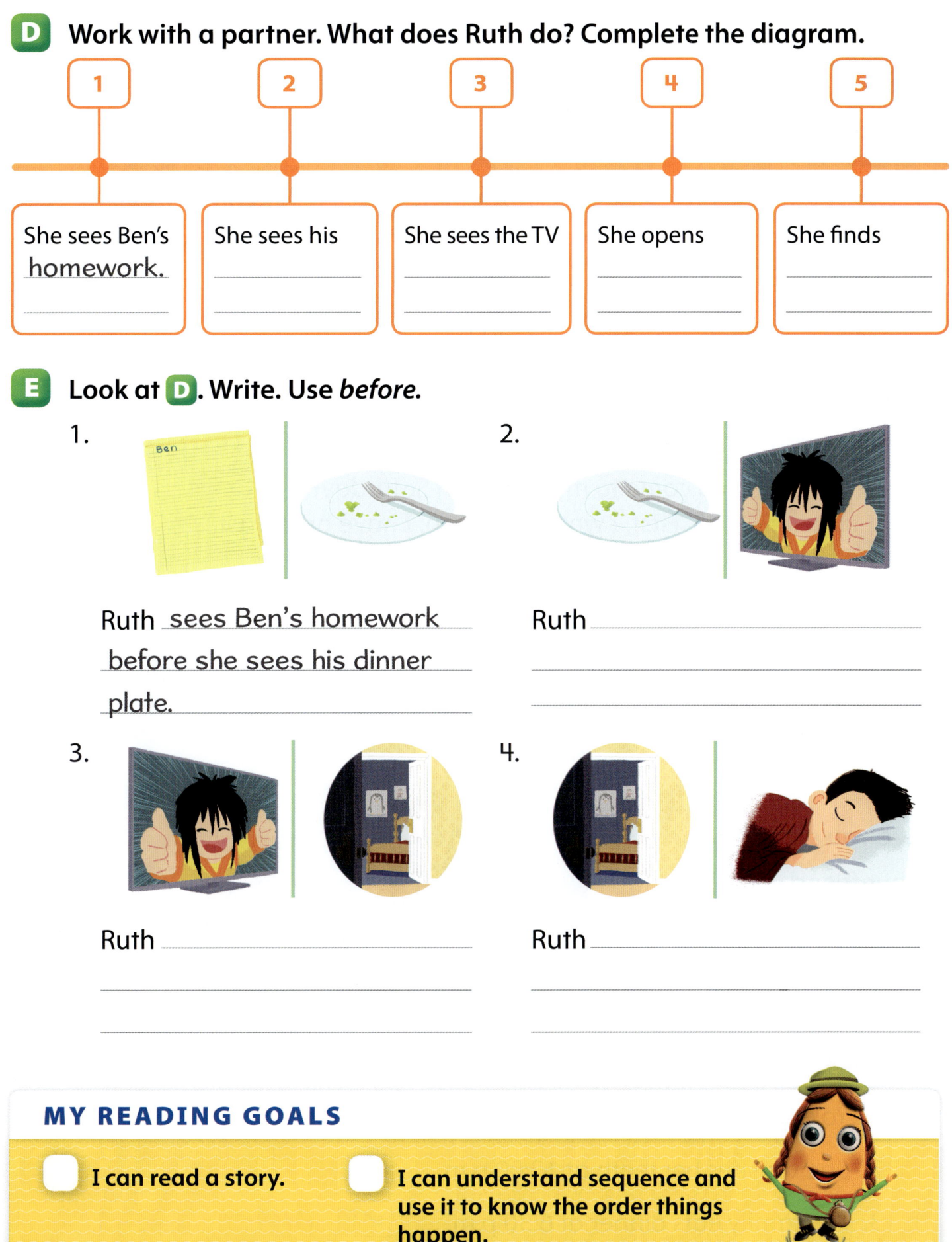

MY READING GOALS

☐ I can read a story.

☐ I can understand sequence and use it to know the order things happen.

Reading Check

Remember!
Find the **times**. When do things happen? Understand the **sequence**. In what order do they happen?

A Read and listen. 🔊 43

Hello Liz,

How are you?

What time can you come to my house on Saturday?
I get up at 8:00 a.m. First, I watch TV. Then, I have breakfast.
Next, I brush my teeth. Come after 9:30 a.m., OK?

We have lunch at 12:00 p.m.! We can have sandwiches for lunch.

We eat dinner at 6:30 p.m. Do you like pasta?

See you soon! Yay!

Your friend,

Yoko

B Look at the times. Choose ✔ or ✘.

1. Yoko gets up at 8:00 a.m. ✔ ✘

2. She brushes her teeth at 12:00 p.m. ✔ ✘

3. Her family eats dinner at 6:30 p.m. ✔ ✘

C Look at the sequence words. Why is the sequence of Yoko's day important? Choose ✔ or ✘.

1. It tells Liz the dinner food. ☑✔ ⊗✘

2. It shows Liz the plan for the day. ☑✔ ☐✘

3. It gives Liz a schedule for school. ☑✔ ☐✘

D Choose the correct answer.

1. Yoko _____ before breakfast.
   ☑ a. watches TV   ☐ b. does homework

2. Yoko wants Liz to come _____ 9:30 a.m.
   ☐ a. before   ☐ b. after

3. They have sandwiches for _____
   ☐ a. lunch.   ☐ b. breakfast.

4. Yoko eats dinner at _____
   ☐ a. 6:30 p.m.   ☐ b. 8:00 p.m.

E Unscramble and match.

1. s r b h e s u r h e e t t e h   •   • Yoko does this at 6:30 p.m.

   __brushes her teeth__

2. o s d e e h k w m r o o   •   • Yoko does this after she watches TV.

   _____

3. s h a k t e f s b a r a   •   • Yoko does this after breakfast.

   _____

4. t e a s n d e i r n   •   • Yoko doesn't do this on Saturday.

   _____

Get Ready to Write

WRITING GOAL: Write a Schedule

A schedule shows what you do at different times in a day.

A Read Hyun-Woo's schedule. Underline the morning times.
Circle the afternoon and evening times.

Writing Tip
Use *a.m.* for times in the morning and *p.m.* for times in the afternoon and evening.

Monday, October 5

7:00 a.m.	get up	7:00 p.m.	have dinner
7:30 a.m.	have breakfast	7:30 p.m.	do homework
8:00 a.m.	brush my teeth	8:00 p.m.	go to bed

B Look at **A**. What does Hyun-Woo do on Monday?
Complete the diagram.

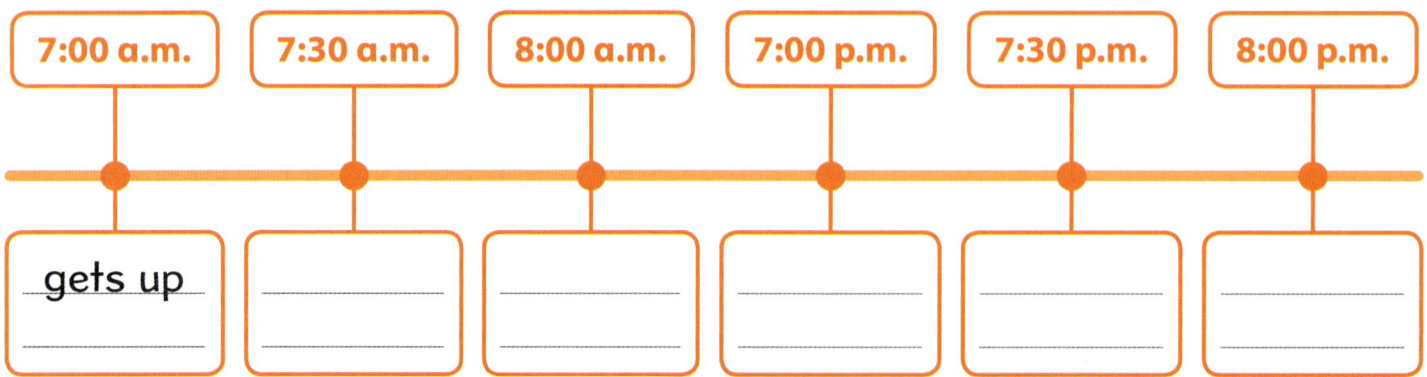

7:00 a.m.	7:30 a.m.	8:00 a.m.	7:00 p.m.	7:30 p.m.	8:00 p.m.
gets up					

Write

C Think about your activities on Monday. Complete the diagram with times and activities.

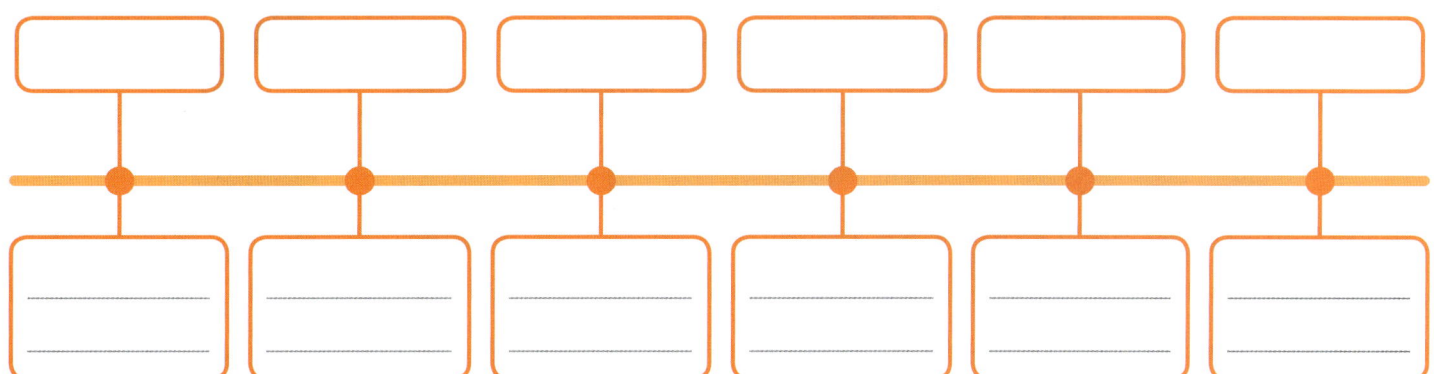

D Now write a schedule. Use your words from **C**.
Choose new words, too. Then draw one of your activities.

Monday

Time	Activity	Time	Activity
a.m.			
		p.m.	

 Now write a schedule about your activities on Saturday.

Reading
with Writing

2

Workbook

Kathryn O'Dell

OXFORD
UNIVERSITY PRESS

Read

READING GOAL:
Read the Title

Remember!
The **title** gives
the topic of
the text.

A Can you find the title? Underline it.

All About Piñatas

This is a picture of a piñata. Piñatas are from Mexico. They are in the United States. They are all around the world.

People make piñatas with paper and glue. They have many shapes. They are circles, stars, and animals.

The piñatas have candy inside them. Some piñatas have crayons and small toys.

Children have piñatas at parties. They are fun! The piñata breaks. Everyone gets candy!

B Read the text. Then choose the correct answer.

1. Where are piñatas from?
   - ☑ a. Mexico
   - ☐ b. the United States
   - ☐ c. around the world

2. What do people use to make piñatas?
   - ☐ a. stars and circles
   - ☐ b. crayons and toys
   - ☐ c. paper and glue

3. What is in a piñata?
   - ☐ a. animals and circles
   - ☐ b. candy and toys
   - ☐ c. paper and glue

4. What's the topic of the text?
   - ☐ a. parties
   - ☐ b. piñatas
   - ☐ c. people

C Trace the words. Then choose the correct picture for each word.

1. _____ picture _____

☐ a. ☑ b.

2. _____ window _____

☐ a. ☐ b.

3. _____ paper clip _____

☐ a. ☐ b.

4. _____ glue _____

☐ a. ☐ b.

D Complete the sentences.

| glue | paper clips | window | ~~picture~~ |

1. This is my _____ picture _____ . It's a bird.

2. I have a _____ in my bedroom.

3. I put a heart on paper with _____

4. I use _____ to put papers together.

E Unscramble and write.

1. l u e g

_____ glue _____

2. r i t p u c e

_____

3. r a p p e c p i l

_____

4. w w n d i o

_____

Read

READING GOAL:
Read the Headings

Remember!
Headings show different parts of a story.

A Can you find the headings? Underline them.

The Friendship Doll

10:00

Today is Saturday. I want to make an art project.
I want to make a picture. My pencil breaks. I use my
pencil sharpener. My pencil breaks again.

10:05

I use yarn for my art project. I make a doll.
My friend Betty comes to my house. I show her
my project.

> **Betty:** Hi, Lucy. That's a cute doll. What's her name?
>
> **Lucy:** Hi, Betty. This is my doll, Mary. How are you?
>
> **Betty:** I'm happy.
>
> **Lucy:** Me too! Let's play!

3:20

Betty sees the clock.

> **Betty:** It's late! I have to go! Goodbye!
>
> **Lucy:** Bye! See you next time!

B Read the story. Then choose **Yes** or **No**.

1. Does Lucy draw a picture?   Yes   (No)
2. Does Lucy use yarn?   Yes   No
3. Does Betty like the doll?   Yes   No
4. Is Betty sad?   Yes   No
5. Do the headings show different times?   Yes   No

C Complete the sentences.

calendar	clock	pencil sharpener	~~yarn~~

1.

This is _____yarn._____

2.

This is my _____

3.

I have a _____

4.

That is a _____

D Complete the sentences.

1. **Jane:** What time is it?

   Paul: I don't know. Look at the _clock._____

2. **Jim:** What day is it?

   Grace: I don't know. Look at the _c_____

3. **Jill:** I need _y_____ for an art project.

   Alex: Here you are.

Write

Circle the names in the conversation below.

Daisy: What's that?

John: It's a calendar.

Read

READING GOAL:
Find Key Information

Remember!
Key information tells you what the text is about.

A Read the e-mail. Think about the key information.

TO: Doug   **FROM:** Carlos

SUBJECT: Internet shopping

Hi Doug,

I like to buy things on the Internet. I go to my favorite Internet store.
I look at the comic books and key chains. I look at the lunch boxes.
I ask Mom, "Can I buy a new lunch box?" She says, "Yes!" I buy the green
lunch box. Now I have a new lunch box.

I really like to buy things on the Internet! What's next?
How about a new orange lunch box for my sister?

Your friend,

Carlos

B Read again. Then choose the correct answer.

1. Where does Carlos shop?

    ☐ a. in a mall   ☑ b. on the Internet   ☐ c. in a toy store

2. What does Carlos buy?

    ☐ a. a comic book   ☐ b. a key chain   ☐ c. a lunch box

3. Who does Carlos send an e-mail to?

    ☐ a. his friend   ☐ b. his dad   ☐ c. his teacher

4. What is the key information?

    ☐ a. Carlos likes key chains.

    ☐ b. Carlos likes to buy things on the Internet.

    ☐ c. Carlos looks at comic books.

C Trace the words. Then choose the correct picture for each word.

1. _____ buy _____   2. _____ comic book _____

☑ a.   ☐ b.   ☐ a.   ☐ b.

3. _____ key chain _____   4. _____ lunch box _____

☐ a.   ☐ b.   ☐ a.   ☐ b.

D Complete the sentences.

| buy | ~~comic books~~ | have | key chain | lunch box | pencil sharpener |

1. I read _____ comic books _____ with my friends.

2. I put a sandwich in my _____

3. I _____ my lunch at school for $3.00.

4. She has three keys on her _____

E Unscramble and write.

1. y b u   2. e k y   h i n a c

_____ buy _____   _____

3. o i c m c   k o b o   4. u l n h c   x o b

_____   _____

Read

READING GOAL: Find the Setting

A Read. Think about where the story happens.

A Gift for Sue

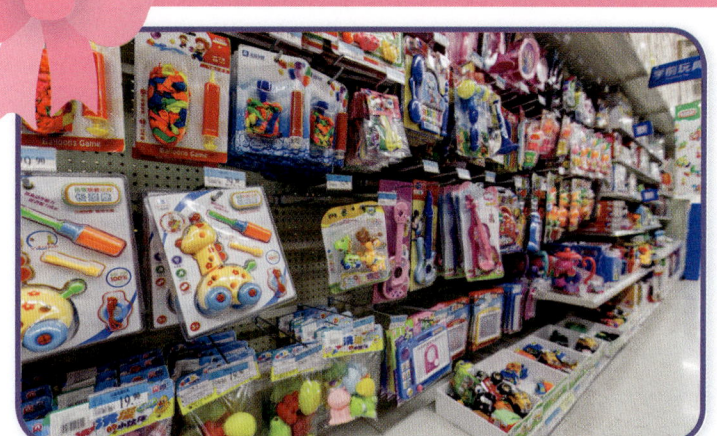

It's Sue's birthday. Mia and her friends shop for Sue. They are in a toy store.

Mia has $5.00. She sees a doll. It's $10.00. Tyron has $5.00 in his wallet. He sees an orange watch. It's $15.00. Carla has $5.00, too. She sees a big action figure. It's $20.00. Oh, no!

What can they buy for Sue? "I know," says Mia. "Let's put our money together." They have $15.00. They buy the orange watch for Sue.

B Read again. Then choose **Yes** or **No**.

1. Is it Mia's birthday?   **Yes**   (**No**)
2. Does Mia have $5.00?   **Yes**   **No**
3. Does Tyron have $15.00?   **Yes**   **No**
4. Does Carla have $20.00?   **Yes**   **No**
5. Does Carla buy an action figure?   **Yes**   **No**
6. Do the friends buy a watch?   **Yes**   **No**
7. Is the setting a toy store?   **Yes**   **No**

C Complete the sentences.

| action figure | candy bar | key chain | wallet | ~~watch~~ | yarn |

1.

I have a purple ___watch.___

2.

I have a _____ in my desk. Yum!

3.

Jill has an _____ in her room.

4.

Rick has a _____ in his bag.

D Complete the paragraph.

This store has a lot of things to buy. I see a cool _watch_____.

It says it's 4:30. I also see an _a_____ _f_____.

She's cool! I see a _w_____ for money. I see a

_c_____ _b_____, too. It's big, and it's only $2.00!

Write

Circle the subject line.

TO: Jen   FROM: Paul

SUBJECT: A shopping trip

Hi Jen. How are you? Can you go shopping today?

Remember!
Choose a word or phrase for the subject line.

Read

READING GOAL:
Find the Action Words

A Read. Think about the actions in the text.

Katie Wins Gym

Katie plays with her friends in gym class. They run on Monday. Katie runs fast. She says, "I win!"

They swim in the pool on Tuesday. Katie swims fast. She says, "I win!"

They play soccer on Wednesday. Katie kicks the ball. She says, "I win!"

They dance on Thursday. Katie dances fast. She says, "I win!"

"Katie!" the gym teacher says. "There isn't a winner! Please just have fun."

They run again on Friday. Katie runs really fast. She says, "This is fun!"

B Read again. Then choose the correct answer.

1. What does Katie do in gym class on Tuesday?

   ☐ a. She runs.   ☑ b. She swims.   ☐ c. She dances.

2. What does the gym teacher tell Katie?

   ☐ a. Have fun.   ☐ b. Run fast.   ☐ c. Kick the ball.

3. What actions does Katie do?

   ☐ a. skips, sings, dances, runs   ☐ b. kicks, swims, dances, buys

   ☐ c. runs, swims, kicks, dances

C Trace the words. Then choose the correct picture for each word.

1. dance

☐ a.   ☑ b.

2. sing

☐ a.   ☐ b.

3. skip

☐ a.   ☐ b.

4. swim

☐ a.   ☐ b.

D Complete the sentences.

| buy | dance | kick | sing | skip | ~~swim~~ |

1. I _____ swim _____ in a pool at my friend's house.

2. We _____ songs in music class.

3. My friends _____ fast at parties.

4. I sometimes _____ to school.

E Unscramble and write.

1. p k i s

_____ skip _____

2. e d c n a

_____

3. m w s i

_____

4. i s n g

_____

Read

READING GOAL:
Find the Main Idea

A Read. Think about the main idea.

Games Around the World

People play games around the world. Hopscotch is from Italy. Children can play hopscotch with nine squares. The squares have numbers in them. The squares are in a line. The squares can be in a circle, too.

Karate is from Japan. Some karate moves are from China. People do karate in many places around the world.

Children jump rope around the world. The game is from the Netherlands. Children can jump rope with one rope. They can jump rope with two ropes, too.

B Read again. Then choose Yes or No.

1. Is hopscotch from China?   Yes   (No)
2. Do kids play hopscotch with nine squares?   Yes   No
3. Is karate from Japan?   Yes   No
4. Is the game jump rope from Italy?   Yes   No
5. Can kids jump rope with two ropes?   Yes   No
6. Is the main idea about games around the world?   Yes   No

C Complete the sentences.

> do karate   jump rope   play hopscotch
>
> play soccer   ~~ride a bike~~   sing a song

1.

   I _____ride a bike_____ to school.

2.

   We _____ on the playground.

3.

   They _____ after school.

4.

   They _____ on Mondays.

D Complete the sentences.

1. We _jump_____ r_____ on the playground.

2. I _p_____ h_____ with my friends.

3. Do you r_____ a b_____ to school?

4. We _d_____ k_____ in gym class.

Remember!
When you write a story, choose a character and a setting.

Write

Circle the character. Underline the setting.

Julia is at school. She plays soccer at lunchtime.

Read

READING GOAL:
Find the Places

A Read. Think about the places in the text.

Helpers

Who helps people? Doctors help sick people. They help people stay healthy, too. They work in hospitals. They work in offices, too. Dentists work in offices. They help people care for their teeth. They clean teeth. They fix teeth, too. Vets work in animal hospitals. They help pets. They help birds and cats. People like vets because they love their pets! Do you help people?

B Read again. Then choose the correct answer.

1. Where do dentists work?
   - ☐ a. in restaurants
   - ☐ b. in schools
   - ☑ c. in offices

2. Who do vets help?
   - ☐ a. doctors
   - ☐ b. pets
   - ☐ c. sick people

3. Why do people like vets?
   - ☐ a. because vets help their pets
   - ☐ b. because vets work in hospitals
   - ☐ c. because vets clean teeth

4. Which place is *not* in the text?
   - ☐ a. restaurants
   - ☐ b. offices
   - ☐ c. animal hospitals

C Trace the words. Then choose the correct picture for each word.

1. _____doctor_____

□ a.   ☑ b.

2. _____dentist_____

□ a.   □ b.

3. _____vet_____

□ a.   □ b.

4. _____cook_____

□ a.   □ b.

D Complete the sentences.

| cook | dentist | ~~doctor~~ | pet | teacher | vet |

1. A _____doctor_____ helps sick people.

2. A _____ helps sick animals.

3. A _____ cleans teeth.

4. A _____ makes food in a restaurant.

E Unscramble and write.

1. t t d n e i s

_____dentist_____

2. k o c o

_____

3. e t v

_____

4. c d o t r o

_____

Read

READING GOAL:
Understand Cause and Effect

A Read. Think about cause and effect.

The First Firefighter

One day, fire falls from the sky and hits the trees. The trees catch fire. People are scared.

Someone says, "Wear these hats." The people wear hard, white hats. They don't get hurt because the fire hits the hats. The hats turn black.

A man in a black hat puts water on the fire. The fire goes out. The people call the man a hero. He becomes a firefighter. Firefighters wear black hats.

B Read again. Then choose **Yes** or **No**.

1. Do the trees catch fire?   (Yes)   No
2. Do the people wear white hats?   Yes   No
3. Do the hats turn green?   Yes   No
4. Does a man cut down the trees?   Yes   No
5. Does a man put out the fire?   Yes   No
6. Do the people think the man is hero?   Yes   No
7. The cause is *fire hits hats*.
   Is *people get hurt* the effect?   **Yes**   No

C Complete the sentences.

| dentist | firefighter | math teacher |
| police officer | soccer player | ~~taxi driver~~ |

1.

A ___taxi driver___
drives in a city.

2.

The _____
kicks the ball in the park.

3.

The _____
wears a red hat.

4.

The _____
helps people in the city.

D Complete the paragraph.

My brother is a __soccer__ __p_____. He runs fast and kicks the
ball. My dad is a __p_____ __o_____. He helps people in our
city. My mom helps people, too. She's a __f_____. I want to be a
__t_____ __d_____. I can drive a yellow car around my city!

Write

Remember!
Use *in* to show where
things happen.

Circle *in* + place in the sentences.

My mom works in a hospital.

We live in South Korea.

Read

READING GOAL:
Find Likes and Dislikes

Remember!
Likes and **dislikes** show how people feel about things.

A **Read. Think about what the people like and dislike.**

Ray's Place

by Vicky Smith

Ray's Place is new. It has good food! I like the sandwiches. I like the burgers, too. You can have cheese on the sandwiches. You can have cheese on the burgers, too. I like cheese on sandwiches, but I don't like cheese on burgers. The restaurant has cake, too. It doesn't have chocolate cake. It has lemon cake. I like lemon cake. It's good at Ray's Place!

B **Read again. Then choose the correct answer.**

1. What cake does Ray's Place have?
   - ☑ a. lemon cake
   - ☐ b. chocolate cake
   - ☐ c. lemon and chocolate cake

2. What is Ray's Place?
   - ☐ a. a school
   - ☐ b. a pizza place
   - ☐ c. a restaurant

3. How does Vicky feel about the sandwiches at Ray's Place?
   - ☐ a. She likes them.
   - ☐ b. She doesn't like them.
   - ☐ c. She doesn't say.

4. Does Vicky like cheese on burgers?
   - ☐ a. Yes, she does.
   - ☐ b. No, she doesn't.
   - ☐ c. She doesn't say.

C Trace the words. Then choose the correct picture for each word.

1. cheese

☐ a.   ✔ b.

2. burger

☐ a.   ☐ b.

3. grapes

☐ a.   ☐ b.

4. sandwich

☐ a.   ☐ b.

D Complete the sentences.

| cake | cheese | burgers | grapes | juice | sandwich |

1. I like green and red _____ grapes. _____

2. We make _____ at home. We put cheese on them.

3. Do you want a _____ or pizza for dinner?

4. I like yellow _____

E Unscramble and write.

1. a h i d w c s n

   _____ sandwich _____

2. s e h e c e

   _____

3. r s g e p a

   _____

4. r g r u b e

   _____

Read

READING GOAL:
Find What Is Similar and Different

A Read. Think about the things that are similar and different.

Lunch in the Park?

Tara and Ian are at home with Mom and Dad on Saturday. "Let's have lunch in the park," Dad says.

They make sandwiches. Tara makes a big cheese sandwich. Ian makes a small cheese sandwich. Mom makes a steak sandwich, and Dad makes a steak sandwich, too. They put their sandwiches in a bag with some cold pasta, four apples, and grapes. They go to the park.

"Oh, no!" Tara says. "The food is at home!"

They go back home. They're hungry! They eat their food at the table.

B Read again. Then choose **Yes** or **No.**

1. Do Ian and Tara both have cheese sandwiches? (Yes) **No**
2. Are Ian and Tara's sandwiches both big? **Yes** **No**
3. Is the pasta hot? **Yes** **No**
4. Does the family go to the park? **Yes** **No**
5. Do they eat at the park? **Yes** **No**
6. Are Mom's and Dad's sandwiches different? **Yes** **No**

C Complete the sentences.

| pasta | ~~rice~~ | cheese | steak | stew | burgers |

1.

My brother likes _____rice._____

2.

I don't like _____

3.

I want _____ for lunch.

4.

We like _____

D Complete the paragraph.

I like _____stew_____ with meat and vegetables in it. My brother

likes _p_____ with red sauce. My sister likes white and brown

_r_____. My mom and dad like _s_____, but I don't like it.

Write

Remember!
Use *and* to show things that are similar. Use *but* to show things that are different.

Underline the sentence that shows things that are similar. Circle the sentence that shows things that are different.

I like cheese, but my brother doesn't like it.

Ray's Place has sandwiches, and Food Time has sandwiches, too.

Read

READING GOAL:
Find Times

A Read. Think about when things happen.

Hi Jack,

How are you? My brother and I go to different schools in our new town. We like our new schools. I get up at 7:00 a.m. My brother gets up at 7:30 a.m. We have breakfast at 8:00 a.m. We brush our teeth after breakfast.

I go to school at 8:30 a.m. I take the bus. My brother goes to school at 9:00 a.m. He walks to school. Or he rides his bike.

Say "hi" to Mike. Eva, too!

Your friend,

Lucy

B Read again. Then choose the correct answer.

1. What time does Lucy's brother eat?
   ☐ a. 7:00 a.m.   ☐ b. 7:30 a.m.   ☑ c. 8:00 a.m.

2. How does Lucy get to school?
   ☐ a. She walks.   ☐ b. She rides her bike.   ☐ c. She takes the bus.

3. Who is Jack?
   ☐ a. Lucy's brother   ☐ b. Lucy's friend   ☐ c. Lucy's teacher

4. What do the different times show for Lucy and her brother?
   ☐ a. morning schedule   ☐ b. after-school schedule
   ☐ c. night-time schedule

C Trace the words. Then choose the correct picture for each word.

1. ___get up___

☑ a.   ☐ b.

2. ___brush my teeth___

☐ a.   ☐ b.

3. ___go to school___

☐ a.   ☐ b.

4. ___have breakfast___

☐ a.   ☐ b.

D Complete the sentences.

| brush my teeth | have breakfast | have lunch |
| go to school | ride my bike | ~~get up~~ |

1. I ___get up___ at 7:30 a.m. Good morning!

2. I _____ with a toothbrush.

3. I _____ at 8:00 a.m. in my dad's car.

4. I _____ in the school café at 8:30 a.m.

E Unscramble and write.

1. a v e h   a t b s a e f k r
   ___have breakfast___

2. o g   o t   c o s l o h
   _____

3. e t g   p u
   _____

4. h r b s u   y m   e t t e h
   _____

Read

READING GOAL:
Understand the Sequence

Remember!
The **sequence** is the order things happen.

A Read the story. Think about the sequence.

A Superhero's Day

This is Jane. She's a girl. She's a superhero, too!

She gets up at 6:00 a.m. First, she has breakfast. Then, she brushes her teeth. Next, she goes to school. She is Jane at school.

She is not Jane after school. She is a superhero. She helps people in the city.

She gets home at 8:00 p.m. and eats dinner. Next, she does her homework. Finally, she goes to bed.

Whew! It's a long day for a student and a superhero.

B Read again. Then choose Yes or No.

1. Does Jane brush her teeth before breakfast?   Yes   (No)

2. Does Jane go to school?   Yes   No

3. Does Jane help people?   Yes   No

4. Does Jane have dinner at home?   Yes   No

5. Does Jane do her homework before dinner?   Yes   No

6. Is the sequence of Jane's day like other kids at school?   Yes   No

C Complete the sentences.

does homework	plays hopscotch	~~eats dinner~~
eats lunch	goes to bed	watches TV

1.
He _____eats dinner_____ at 6:30 p.m.

2.
She _____ after school.

3.
He _____ before dinner.

4.
She _____ at 9:00 p.m.

D Complete the paragraph.

I _do_ h_____ after school. I h_____ d_____
with my family at 5:30 p.m. I w_____ T_____ before bed.
I g_____ t_____ b_____ at 8:30 p.m.

Write

Circle the times.

I get up at 7:30 a.m., and I have breakfast at 8:00 a.m.

She does her homework at 4:00 p.m.

> **Remember!**
> Use *a.m.* for times in the morning and *p.m.* for times in the afternoon and evening.

Picture Dictionary

Write the key words.

Unit 1

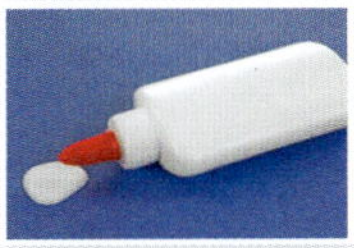

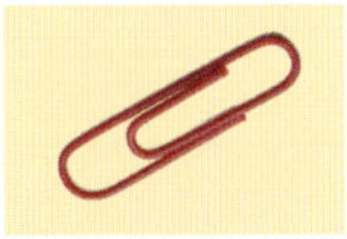

_____

_____

_____

_____

Unit 2

_____

_____

_____

_____

Unit 3

_____

_____

_____

_____

Unit 4

_____

_____

_____

_____

Picture Dictionary

Unit 5

_____
_____

_____
_____

_____
_____

_____
_____

Unit 6

_____
_____

_____
_____

_____
_____

_____
_____

Unit 7

_____
_____

_____
_____

_____
_____

_____
_____

Unit 8

_____
_____

_____
_____

_____
_____

_____
_____

Unit 9

_____

_____

_____

_____

Unit 10

_____

_____

_____

_____

Unit 11

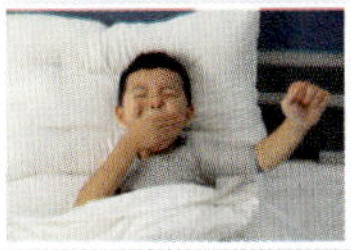

_____

_____

_____

_____

Unit 12

_____

_____

_____

_____

Syllabus

Topic	Unit	Reading Goal	Key Words	Writing Goal
TOPIC 1 Art Smart	Unit 1	Read the Title	*picture, glue, paper clip, window*	Write a Conversation
	Unit 2	Read the Headings	*calendar, pencil sharpener, clock, yarn*	Focus: Names and capital letters
TOPIC 2 My Shopping Trip	Unit 3	Find Key Information	*buy, key chain, lunch box, comic book*	Write an E-mail
	Unit 4	Find the Setting	*action figure, watch, wallet, candy bar*	Focus: Description words
TOPIC 3 Fun and Games	Unit 5	Find the Action Words	*swim, dance, skip, sing*	Write a Story
	Unit 6	Find the Main Idea	*jump rope, play hopscotch, do karate, ride a bike*	Focus: Character and setting
TOPIC 4 My Heroes	Unit 7	Find the Places	*cook, dentist, doctor, vet*	Write a Paragraph
	Unit 8	Understand Cause and Effect	*soccer player, taxi driver, police officer, firefighter*	Focus: *In* to show location
TOPIC 5 Yum!	Unit 9	Find Likes and Dislikes	*sandwich, burger, cheese, grapes*	Write an Opinion
	Unit 10	Find What Is Similar and Different	*steak, stew, rice, pasta*	Focus: Conjunctions *and* and *but*
TOPIC 6 My Day	Unit 11	Find Times	*get up, have breakfast, brush your teeth, go to school*	Write a Schedule
	Unit 12	Understand the Sequence	*do homework, eat dinner, watch TV, go to bed*	Focus: Time abbreviations *a.m.* and *p.m.*